Make Your Own Waves

OrangeBooks Publication

1st Floor, Rajhans Arcade, Mall Road, Kohka, Bhilai, Chhattisgarh 490020

Website: www.orangebooks.in

© Copyright, 2025, Author

All rights reserved. No part of this book may be reproduced, stored in a retrieval system, or transmitted, in any form by any means, electronic, mechanical, magnetic, optical, chemical, manual, photocopying, recording or otherwise, without the prior written consent of its writer.

First Edition, 2025

ISBN: 978-93-6554-358-2

MAKE YOUR OWN WAVES

Gaurav Krishnan

OrangeBooks Publication
www.orangebooks.in

Dedication

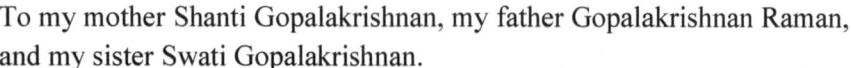

To my mother Shanti Gopalakrishnan, my father Gopalakrishnan Raman, and my sister Swati Gopalakrishnan.

Also dedicated to my grandmother Smt. Kamala Sankaranarayanan (1943-2023) and my grandfather P.A. Raman (1913-1995).

About

This book was written with the aim of reaching people in whatever time or place to provide fuel to the burning fire of questioning our purpose and our place here on this "mote of dust suspended on a sunbeam" as Carl Sagan suggested in his 'Pale Blue Dot' analogy. We're on this piece of rock rotating around its axis, and revolving around the Sun and are perhaps the only intelligent life in a seemingly boundless universe… perhaps.

Yet the human condition requires us to go deeper into what's inside us and what's around us to make sense of this brief period of a lifespan we occupy in our place in the cosmos. It's fleeting at best, but in these chapters, I'll explore knowledge and ideas spanning the ages of human existence to provide as a blueprint of how to live thoughtfully, mindfully and fully present and wholesomely.

To answer the burgeoning questions of how to live, what to pursue and how to live a fulfilled life are the core ingredients that stride the chapters of this book.

This book is a collection of all the perspectives, ideas and questions I've come across over the years as I've grown from a teenager and my 20s living fast and hard, immersed headlong into the breach, to my more contemplative 30s where I've yearned for a quiet, calm and contemplative reflection of looking back at the past, learning from it and searching for answers and meaning that could shape the future.

My journey through life has been quite unconventional, yet I've taken it in my stride and have come across some profound perspectives that have altered how I view life and which have led to some moving and deeply meaningful changes in the way I live.

This is my third book, after releasing two poetry books called *The Indian Night* in 2022 and another book on beat poetry of the 21st century called *Interludes To The Indian Buddha* in 2023. In both those books I turned to poetry as the way to express myself and offer my unique perspective in poetic verses.

This book however, is a contrasting shift because it's my first full length book that isn't poetry but a call to arms for the thinkers, doers, dreamers, misfits and everybody and anybody who questions life deeply. This is my latest work alongside my explorations as a musician under my stage name *Ghost Intent* and as a singer songwriter and film composer.

The hope is that with this book, I can empower more people to see outside the regular ways they view the world and urge a deeper connection with themselves and offer a fresh viewpoint on life and existence.

Thank you for purchasing my book and I hope it helps you in whatever way it can to lead to breakthroughs and in living a more fulfilled life.

Preface

This book is for anybody and everybody willing to ask the big questions about existence and why we're here and how the best way to go about "propagating our lust for life", as The Doors frontman Jim Morrison wrote in his poetry works. In these chapters you'll uncover some eyeopening perspectives that challenge the norm and that have been handed down through the centuries offering unique viewpoints on life and the human condition.

Within the hallways of the chapters of this book you'll find ideas, philosophies and perspectives that will urge you to think and rethink and urge a sense of change from the usual and break out into a more fulfilled life and existence.

In essence, this book could be called a 'book of books' of sorts or a book encompassing perspectives that cover all the most intriguing concepts I've read about in other books or on the internet — ones that have deeply moved me or led to a rethink on life and how to live it. These perspectives have come together rather fittingly like the perfect pieces that fit the puzzle and are a roadmap for you to uncover step by step as you turn through the pages and chapters.

In these chapters you'll find some of the most prominent thinkers and people who have pushed and probed into the unknown to uncover the hidden goodness and richness of life, beyond societal norms and usual ways of living it.

This culmination of concepts, ideas and perspectives will urge you to think and help you break out of the usual & mundane and in essence, think about life differently.

From existentialist dilemmas, self-improvement, and purpose and meaning, to scientific studies and spiritual pursuits and philosophy, culture and history, this book covers a wide range of ideas that I've tried to fit in together, like a perfect edit of a film, shot in a non-linear fashion, to jump back and forth between concepts that will urge you to rethink the way you live life, and foster a more meaningful and enriched living experience.

These are questions that have puzzled the greatest thinkers through time, but this book is my quiet and brief attempt at addressing them and fitting them all together into a short book that you can read at leisure or by a pristine view, that could lead to some essential breakthroughs or simply feed the intellect and search for meaning.

So, wherever you are in time, picking up this book, here's a blueprint for you break the shackles of the mundane and usual, to rethink how you view life, and of course, with a pause, a crash and a hiss… empower you to make your own waves…

Table of Contents

1. Four Thousand Leagues Ltd. 1
2. Albert Camus & The Absurd 4
3. To Float or Swim? —Hunter S. Thompson's Letter 8
4. Schopenhauer's Thought & Solving the Paradox 12
5. Defining Success 15
6. Mindset Is Everything 18
7. Balance & Wu Wei – From Alan Watts to Ramana Maharshi & Stoicism 21
8. Eckhart Tolle on Living in The Moment & Jiddu Krishnamurti on Fear 26
9. A Modern Take on Self-Inquiry & What Spirituality Is 30
10. Bukowski's Words on Passion 34
11. Make Room for Art in Your Life 37
12. It's Never Too Late to Start 44
13. How To Make Hard Choices 47
14. This Is Water —David Foster Wallace's Message 51
15. Everyone Is on A Different Journey, So Stop Comparing 55
16. Still Water — A Zen Parable on How to Achieve a Peaceful State of Mind 59
17. Learn The Lessons of The Past 62
18. Nature Therapy 65
19. Travelling Is the Best Use of Time & Money 67
20. Ikigai & Other Japanese Concepts 71
21. This Is Sparta! 74
22. The 2x Value Principle —Create Value in Your Work & Value Your Work 77
23. Think of a Problem, Engineer A Solution 79

24.	Education Doesn't Matter, Skills Do 81
25.	Start Where You Are with What You Have 84
26.	Perseverance & Grit Will See You Through 87
27.	Response To Failure Is Paramount - An Exploration By Robert H. Schuller 90
28.	La Pausa: The Importance of Pause 95
29.	No Risk, No Reward Lessons Learned From 'The Big Short' 101
30.	Practice, Practice, Practice - How Habits Make You & Why Practice Is Essential 106
31.	Standing On The Shoulder of Giants — Not Oasis But Sir Isaac Newton 111
32.	Immanuel Kant On Learning & Spreading Knowledge 115
33.	Disruption & Problem Solving 119
34.	Teamwork & Ditching the Limelight 122
35.	Some Drugs Help Explore What's Within, Make It An Experience Not A Habit 126
36.	Connect The Dots: The Steve Jobs Perspective 128
37.	Live Below Your Means, Be Humble & Don't Be A Victim Of Consumerism 130
38.	The Road Less Traveled Robert Frost's Poem 134
39.	Invent Yourself, & Keep Reinventing Yourself 139
40.	The Reward Is To Play & Mushin — The Flow State 144
41.	Family & Relationships Keep Us Happy & Healthy 149
42.	About Coping with Loss 151
43.	Live By a Code 155
44.	In The End, It Doesn't Matter Whether You Get Rich or Not But How Fulfilled Your Life Is 157
45.	Leave A Legacy 160

Four Thousand Leagues Ltd.

Starting a book can be daunting, writing a book is even more terrifying. A deft hook for starters or a catchy way to begin a book may be aplenty in the history of writing, but by starting this book in this way, I wanted to create awareness & understanding. Moreover, I wanted the data point I mention below to serve as the basis & the first section that outlines why this book could help you & serve as your guideline in the ever-hyper-speed 2020s.

This particular statistic may scare you. It may also lead you to a moment of realisation or a brief epiphany on truly understanding how short our time living life here on Earth is.

There's this famous song by the Britpop band The Verve that goes, "It's a bittersweet symphony, that's life. Trying to make ends meet, you're a slave to money then you die." — it's a pretty grim but reflective bit of songwriting and a cool song nonetheless.

"I don't have the time" or in Hindi "mere paas time nahi hai", you've probably heard people say this all the time, but what are they or you, truly spending your time on? There's also of course the "time is money" proverb, but 'time' is worth much more than trading it off inconsequentially for or in search of money. You may have heard that time is your most valuable resource… a lot… but, until it hits you & you truly understand how little time you have, you'll keep squandering it away.

The average life span for human beings is roughly only about 4000 weeks as explored by Oliver Burkeman in his book titled *Four Thousand Weeks: Time Management For Mortals — Time and How to Use It*. It quantified the shocking yet blunt truth, that that's all the time you have to live, give or take — 4000 weeks.

That statistic hit me really hard. Life is so short & fragile, so how you spend your time is paramount. Time is your most valuable resource, and you just have 4000 weeks, that's it, 4000 weeks assuming you live until you're 76.

"Arguably, time management is all life is. Yet the modern discipline known as time management — like its hipper cousin, productivity — is a depressingly narrow-minded affair, focused on how to crank through as many work tasks as possible", says Oliver Burkeman.

Some key points to note are:

i) **The obsession with being productive & accruing wealth has made it difficult for people to appreciate family & personal time**

Spending time with family & personal time should be the most important thing in life, yet the way the world works and the way society is constructed entails that we must trade it for work & productivity. Despite our work obligations it's of utmost importance to ensure we spend more time with our family and loved ones & also to make room for personal time & space.

It's far more important, healthy & necessary. Considering we just have 4000 weeks to live give or take, instead of 'work' coming first, 'family & personal time' should be prioritised in our weekly schedule. So if you're making a daily or weekly planner, schedule family time first, and keep work for after it.

ii) **The best way to make the most of our time is to spend it doing the things we love**

Balancing our work with what we actually *want* to do is the key. Start doing more things you've always wanted to or really want to do; the rest can come later. Furthermore, aligning your work with what you love to do is a great way to feel more fulfilled.

There's a story about Warren Buffet & his pilot where Buffet asked his pilot to list down a list of the top 25 things he desired. After that, Buffet told his pilot to rank them in order of importance & then suggested that he should do the top 5 things & ditch all the rest. So do something similar, and do those top 5 or 10 things you truly want to do.

Even in our free time, we need to allocate more time to doing projects & things we feel we really *want* to do. So, watch that movie with your family, take your kids outside for a picnic, spend quality time with your spouse, and pursue your hobbies & passions, whatever they may be.

iii) Procrastination is a natural and healthy human behaviour

Many of us recognise the tendency to postpone our duties, but procrastination is a natural human inclination that we cannot avoid. Therefore, we must shift our attention from striving to get everything done and prioritising what is most important to embracing procrastination as a natural human tendency. While procrastination does seem like an evil, it really isn't.

We don't 'have' to do a lot of things, at times just sitting back enjoying the view on your travels at a cafe or in an Airbnb balcony or in your garden sitting on your porch sipping a coffee or simply doing nothing is perfectly fine. Doing nothing is absolutely fine and needs to be normalised. Procrastination isn't an evil but a natural way for our mind and body to reset.

iv) Pay yourself first

Paying yourself first is originally a financial concept, but we can use it for time management. Instead of waiting for a free slot of time, we can create time in our calendar to focus on paying ourselves first with the things we want to do & then do everything else. Making more room for doing what you want to do, and less with what your job entails, is healthy and fulfilling.

v) Paying attention to how we spend our days is the most effective method for choosing what to accomplish with our time

According to cosmic insignificance therapy, we are insignificant in the larger scheme of the universe. It makes no difference whether we have the ability of Mozart or Albert Einstein; in the perspective of the cosmos, doing whatever makes us happy is the most worthwhile and best way to spend our 4,000 weeks.

Life is short, so it's paramount that we spend our days doing the things we want to do, and make more time for it on a consistent basis. In the end, how we spend our 4000 weeks, makes our lifetime.

Gaurav Krishnan

Albert Camus & The Absurd

"Man stands face to face with the irrational. He feels within him his longing for happiness and for reason. The absurd is born of this confrontation between the human need and the unreasonable silence of the world." — Albert Camus, The Myth of Sisyphus

It's rather paradoxical that the fabled writer Albert Camus contrived to die in a car crash in Villeblevin with a train ticket in his pocket which he decided not to use at the very last minute. It was an untimely event that took place on the 4th of January 1960, when a Facel Vega sports car driven by publisher Michel Gallimard en route to Paris smashed into a tree in the tiny French town of Villeblevin, in Burgundy.

Gallimard died five days later in hospital, but his wife and daughter somehow miraculously survived. The passenger in the front seat, a 46-year-old Albert Camus, however, died instantly. In his coat pocket was the train ticket to Paris which he decided against using and in the boot was the first 144 handwritten pages of his unfinished autobiographical novel, *The First Man*.

This abrupt and seemingly absurd event aligns almost uncannily with the ideas Camus explored in his body of work. His novels—*The Stranger* (1942), *The Plague* (1947), *The Fall* (1956)—and philosophical essays like *The Myth of Sisyphus* (1942) and *The Rebel* (1951) became foundational in his exploration of the Absurd. His characters often faced situations that mirrored his philosophical views, where human longing for meaning collided with the unending silence of the universe.

"What is the meaning of life?", "Why are we here?", "What is our purpose?", these existential questions often arise over the course of our lifetime, but Camus' philosophy of Absurdism suggests that **there is no real answer** & that the only true recognition is that there is **no higher meaning beyond what we decide for ourselves.**

Camus suggested that "It is absurd to continually seek meaning in life when there is none". It's at this crossroads of wanting & searching for meaning but there being no such thing, that our free will to do as we please & our desire to want some kind of reward in the form of finding meaning or purpose, serves as ephemeral brain & soul fodder subjectively creating a made-up idea to define or drive our existence.

Despite finding meaning and a purpose, a 'why?' to drive our existence & lives, the plain matter of fact is that there is no 'why?', and that it's entirely made up by us as a reason to drive our lives in this fragile timeframe of existence. These purposes & reasons we attach to ourselves are entirely made by us & there is no grander meaning, in truth, apart from what we align with ourselves.

This is where Camus presents a core idea: the human compulsion to seek meaning is in itself absurd because life inherently has no meaning. Yet, it is this search for purpose in a purposeless universe, that our free will comes into play. We try to create meaning, either through action, work, or belief, even though none of it is truly validated by the indifferent silence of existence. That is essentially where we grapple with the truth of absurdity.

We confront absurdity every time we ask ourselves the question, "What is the purpose of life?" But Camus rejects traditional answers to this question— whether they come from religion, science, or philosophy—as mere illusions. **These constructed meanings are human responses to the absurd,** nothing more, he suggests.

It's from this tension that Camus argues we must derive our own way of living. Though life holds no inherent meaning, we as humans are free to create our own subjective interpretations of existence. Some people may find solace in art, work, or personal relationships, while others may embrace creativity or success.

Absurdism tells us that we cannot help but question our existence, but we must simultaneously reject the idea that there's a grand answer. There's no scientific, spiritual, or philosophical truth waiting to be discovered. All we have is the subjective meaning we create for ourselves, born from the raw confrontation with the absurd. We live, we search for meaning, we face life's futility and we carry on, knowing that the answer may never come.

You could write a book about it in itself, but comparing Camus' philosophy to Eastern thought, Camus' philosophy of Absurdism and the concept of *dharma* in Hinduism offer two distinct approaches to life's meaning and purpose.

Camus argues that life is inherently meaningless, and any search for a higher purpose is futile. He suggests that the human condition is one of absurdity caught between a deep desire for meaning and the cold, indifferent universe. In response, he advocates for **embracing this absurdity by living in alignment with our innate design & individuality** and creating individual meaning despite the lack of any grander purpose.

On the other hand, *dharma* in Hinduism refers to a person's duty, righteousness, and the grander order of the universe.

It implies that every individual has a specific higher role and purpose aligned with the greater cosmic order, and fulfilment comes through living in accordance with one's *dharma*.

Unlike Camus, who rejects the idea of an inherent meaning, Hinduism holds that *dharma* provides a structured path for life, guiding actions in harmony with spiritual and cosmic principles. However, whether you choose to believe in *dharma* or not, the fact remains that it's a human-made construct we're using to give ourselves meaning. Being raised in a Hindu household myself, I often grappled with these concepts, but in the end, it seems that Camus' Absurdism held a cornerstone of truth to it — that *dharma* **is just an idea of 'meaning' we've attached to the true meaninglessness of life & the universe**.

While comparing Absurdism to Buddhism and Taoism, Camus' philosophy of Absurdism shares some similarities with both schools of thought. Both acknowledge the impermanence and inherent suffering of life, but while Camus advocates **embracing the absurd** and **creating personal meaning despite it**, Eastern philosophies often suggest **transcending the need for meaning altogether.**

Buddhism teaches the cessation of suffering through detachment from desires, while Taoism encourages harmony with the natural flow of existence, accepting life's inherent unpredictability without resistance.

Camus' **call to live authentically despite absurdity** parallels the Eastern emphasis on presence and acceptance, but where Camus urges rebellion against meaninglessness, Eastern philosophies tend toward living in detachment & creating inner peace through surrender.

However, in a way, Camus' philosophy can be considered as having a pervading truth to it because following *dharma* or Buddhism or Taoism is just meaning we've attached to our lives in the midst of the void — a meaning attached to the absurd.

For Camus, **the Absurd isn't about resignation** but about **living authentically in spite of it**. In living as authentically as we can, being true to ourselves (just as Hunter S. Thompson urges in the next chapter) we can choose to do as we please, and it is in this choice, whether we attach meaning to it or not, that Camus suggests is a victory in itself i.e. to live as authentically, staying true to our core being & not being swayed by what others & society may deem as our roles & purposes.

That was the core of his philosophy—embracing life for what it is, knowing there is no ultimate meaning beyond what we give it, **but in response, to live authentically despite it.**

You may find the contents of this book slightly contradictory to this chapter in terms of the ideas I've stated about finding meaning & fulfilment, but the key concept I try to bring to the forefront is that you **need to live in alignment with your individuality & what you individually want to strive towards.**

Finding meaning & purpose is great, at times even pivotal, but you must understand that it isn't some higher purpose; it's just a reason we choose to give ourselves, a 'why?' that we attach in confrontation with the absurd.

It's about choosing to live without illusions, understanding that the absurd is not to be escaped but faced head-on. There is no higher truth, no grand design, only the choices we make in this fleeting moment of existence & our lifetime — it's our decision.

To Float or Swim? —Hunter S. Thompson's Letter

At just 22 years old, notorious journalist and public figure, Hunter S. Thompson penned a profound letter to his friend Hume Logan, who had sought his advice on life.

If you're unfamiliar with Hunter S. Thompson, he was an American journalist and writer, known for his unorthodox approach to both his craft and his life. His bold & unique worldview, later defined as "gonzo" journalism, was evident even in his early years. This candid letter, written long before his rise to fame and notoriety, offers an evocative and deeply insightful perspective on finding one's purpose and leading a life of meaning or to just, as he puts it, 'float'.

Thompson reflects on the concept of living a life of fulfilment, whether by setting and chasing goals or by being content with the present, free from the burden of a predefined path. For those who choose to pursue goals, he emphasises the importance of **finding goals that align with our individuality**, rather than conforming to society's expectations. Our goals, according to Thompson, should be pursued within the scope of our abilities and desires.

In his letter to his friend Hume Logan, Hunter S. Thompson explores one of the deepest existential dilemmas we face in life: the choice between "floating" and "swimming." Should we allow ourselves to drift along the currents of circumstance, living life freely from one day to the next enjoying each moment without a predefined path to follow? Or should we consciously swim, actively steering toward a chosen goal? At its core, this metaphor addresses how we navigate our journey through life.

Thompson starts out his letter exploring the perils of seeking advice on life from others. Even my advice in this book should be just a guiding path, and you must choose to follow what resonates with you. This is because everybody's life is shaped by their unique experiences, desires, and perspectives, so no advice can universally apply.

Each of us must face the essential existential question: "to float or swim?"

The choice, as Thompson puts it, is one we all make consciously or unconsciously at some point in life. *Floating* means going with the flow, perhaps enjoying life without a clear purpose or goal and living one day to the next in contentment. It's not wrong to live freely & float, it's just another way to live life.

Swimming, on the other hand, involves setting a direction, path & goal and making a concerted effort to reach it. Thompson doesn't dismiss floating entirely. If you don't have a clear goal, he suggests, it might be better to enjoy the ride than struggle in uncertainty. However, for those who seek meaning and direction, *floating* can quickly become stagnation, leaving you disillusioned and dissatisfied.

The difficulty arises when we try to define that goal, Thompson argues. Many of us fall into the trap of seeking a "big rock candy mountain," an idealised, fantastical goal with no real substance. Thompson argues that the real tragedy in life is **focusing too much on the goal itself rather than on the person striving for it.**

As we grow and evolve, our desires and perspectives change. The goals we once held may tend to lose their relevance, not because the goals change, but because we do. Therefore, adjusting our lives to meet a fixed goal can lead to frustration.

Instead of chasing a specific outcome, Thompson encourages finding a way of life that aligns with who we are in our core being and what it means to us. This means shaping a life that allows us to express our abilities and fulfil our desires, rather than moulding ourselves to meet the demands of an external goal.

It's not about becoming a doctor, businessman, fireman, or banker for the sake of those titles—it's about choosing a path that **lets you function authentically**, one where your growth, creativity, and self-expression are fully realised. The goal itself becomes secondary to the process of living in alignment with your true self.

Thompson's insight is particularly poignant when he talks about the danger of predefined paths. Society often presents us with a narrow set of choices— careers, lifestyles, or societal roles—that we're expected to follow. If none of these options feel right, Thompson urges us to "find a ninth path."

It's not an easy task, as many of us lead vertical lives, narrowly focused on a limited range of experiences. However, if we procrastinate, avoiding the hard work of choosing our own path, life will inevitably make the choice for us, he suggests.

Thompson makes it clear that this search is not about chasing a singular, grand goal. Rather, it's about crafting a way of life that brings satisfaction, where we can live a life that aligns with our abilities and desires. We should strive to live in a way that brings authenticity and allows us to function at our highest potential. It's a warning to avoid letting others define your goals for you, as that would strip away one of the most important aspects of life: the freedom to choose your own way.

Thompson writes that this is his personal view, shaped by his own experiences, and may not resonate with everyone. But his broader message, however, is that life doesn't have to follow the predetermined paths society presents. You have the power to forge your own road, to live a life that is meaningful to you, even if it requires going against the tide of what's expected of you.

In a world where people often feel trapped by circumstance or the expectations of others, Thompson's letter offers a liberating message at the heart of it. He argues that you don't have to float aimlessly through life, nor must you swim toward someone else's idea of success. Instead, you can chart a course that truly reflects who you are and what you want.

Make Your Own Waves

According to me, life is comprised of both *floating* and *swimming*. Yes, we have our long or medium-term goals but the process of living life until we get there is what makes the experience worth living. So, life, then, is a combination of both *floating* and *swimming*.

We **swim towards our goals** when we need to & we enjoy the balance by **floating through our current situations** by just taking in moments to look at the horizon and the sun setting over the sea, by floating through the little drifts of moments from one day to the next, in essence, to *float* and *swim*.

The choice of deciding what to do when is completely yours, but either way, make sure it's your decision that resonates with you & your individuality and not one handed down by life, society or circumstance.

You can find Thompson's letter online or on my Medium page; it makes for a compelling read.

Schopenhauer's Thought & Solving the Paradox

Throughout history, great thinkers have critically pondered about life and the process of finding and achieving meaning. The tunnel of a lifetime must end with the light of fulfilment… or at least that's the goal. Despite 2500 years of philosophy, the greatest thinkers through history haven't addressed the issue of middle age and the state of being in a mid-life crisis.

The average middle age of a lifetime is the late 30s and early 40s. Most people, when they're young and full of ambition, have goals that must be achieved by that time or are in pursuit of the same goals while they near that age, or on the other hand, have already achieved their intended goals.

However, there is a paradox which suggests that **getting what you want will leave you without purpose**, while **not having it is just as bad because you are left wanting**.

According to German philosopher and pessimist Arthur Schopenhauer who was vociferous on the futility of desire, you're doomed if you achieve your desire or if you don't.

As the case is with any paradox, a delve into philosophy is warranted.

If you get what you want, your pursuit is over. You've reached your goal and life pursuit. You are aimless, flooded with idleness and *ennui* (French for '*boredom*').

As Schopenhauer writes in *The World as Will and Representation (1818)* you are filled with '*fearful emptiness and boredom*', once you've achieved the goals that you've embarked on conquering.

On the other hand, if you still haven't achieved your life goals, projects, desires or ambitions you find yourself trapped in the black hole of wanting that which you do not have, which is suffering.

Just as Buddhism suggests, desire is the cause of suffering. But as human beings, it is difficult to ignore our desires.

Schopenhauer further writes that life *'swings like a pendulum to and from between pain and boredom, and these two are in fact its ultimate constituents'*.

However, Schopenhauer's perspective of boredom and his paradox can be solved. It's not as banal as he portrays it, so there is light at the end of the tunnel.

To explain, a rather surprising look into linguistics has the answer.

The word *'telic'*, derived from *'telos'*, the Greek word for *'purpose'*, defines a *'telic'* activity as **having a definite end** i.e. a terminal state of exhaustion and completion. That's a *'telic'* activity. Which are your goals, desires, ambitions and projects. They are finite and will end with you either achieving them or failing.

Whereas there are *'atelic'* activities which have no finite end. Such as listening to music, or meeting friends, or spending time with family, reading, or travelling. You can stop doing them, but you cannot finish or complete them.

They are never-ending processes. The transient and ephemeral nature of these *'atelic'* activities ensures that they cannot be exhausted. Which means they continue regardless of the outcome of finite activities.

This does not mean that we must abandon our life goals. No, they matter.

It's great to have goals and pursue them, with a focused and at times even relentless demeanour, but as I've explained, be wary of the 4000-week average lifespan.

However, to enjoy **the process** of that pursuit of a *telic* goal with **a series of *atelic* activities** and events on a daily & weekly basis is the key to maintaining a **balance** in our daily lives. That enjoyment of the process solves and separates a mid-life or late-life crisis of having not achieved goals or achieving them and feeling dissatisfied.

So, it's perhaps paramount that we enrich our lives with a combination of *atelic* and *telic* activities.

Enjoy living in the moment with such *atelic* activities, just as Eckhart Tolle puts forth in '*The Power of Now*'. By indulging exponentially in the process of living while also accomplishing your goals, targets, projects and endeavours, in the end, leads to a much more fulfilled life.

To overcome a mid-life crisis or the end of our life goals, we must strike the right chords of **balance** in our daily activities with **both unending activities** and **finite ones** in the persistent pursuit of our defined purposes and lives.

Defining Success

"Define success on your own terms, achieve it by your own rules, and build a life you're proud to live." - Anne Sweeney

Tyler Durden, the fictional character in the movie *Fight Club* probably summed up the 21st-century pipe dream that's bought & sold rather aptly. Whether you've watched *Fight Club* or read the book, Durden is perhaps the one of the few fictional characters who could be taken seriously on his reflective worldview. Success has become a buzzword for accumulating wealth in the 21st century. You'll find thousands of books telling you that success is directly proportional to the money you make in your lifetime.

They'll comprise stories and advice on how to become richer, which is success according to them. You'll also find the media and social media glorifying the richest people around the world as the archetypal definition of success.

This is a concept totally engineered by the West, whereas traditionally, the East reflects on living a more peaceful, meaningful & fulfilled life, irrespective of your financial status.

However, as consumerism emerged in the West & spread across the globe, this concept of success as your net worth, and assets and the amount of money you have in your bank account, has gripped cultures around the world in a stranglehold.

As you'll discover in this book, I often take a contrarian but reflective standpoint on a lot of topics, creating a rhetoric that aligns with what are the ideal ways to live a fulfilling & meaningful life or just providing food for thought.

There are many facets of being a successful person and success is how you define it.

For some, it could be to love and to be loved in return by the people they care about the most. For others, it could be finding peace and contentment. For others, it could be living in their dream location and leading a simple life. For some, it could be graduating from college & finding success in their careers. For some, it could be watching their favourite sports team at their home stadium win a trophy, or for some, mastering a musical instrument and so on.

There are a few kinds of success. Near-term success, medium-term & long-term success.

Near-term success, is when you have, as the name suggests, a short-term goal that you achieve, that's a weekly or monthly target. It can be clearing an exam, acing an interview, running an x amount of kilometres on your weekly or daily run, cooking or ordering that meal you wanted this week for yourself & your family, or dining out at a restaurant on a date, it can be anything that has a target that you've achieved in the near term.

Medium-term success can be a yearly goal or target, such as finishing a course or mastering a certain aspect of a skill, travelling somewhere you want to in the year, or other yearly goals and targets.

Long-term success is when you achieve a goal that takes more than 3-5 years or more. Whether that's using your skills to achieve something that gives you contentment and that you've been wanting to achieve in the timeframe of more than 3 years or more. Such as learning a language, learning a musical instrument, travelling to all the countries on your bucket list, starting a company, or any longer-term goal.

The point is that success is totally subjective from person to person and can't be clubbed into the dank definition of only making more wealth.

If monetary gain is your definition of success, then by all means, let it be. But if it's not, there's a world of possibilities out there with things to do and targets and goals to achieve. In identifying what you'd like to be your definition of success is in the near-term, medium-term or long-term, you can align with what makes you happy and gives you purpose & meaning. This is life, not a race; we're here to live out our 4000 weeks to the fullest. This is not a sprint to a finish line.

Make Your Own Waves

Another aspect I'd like to touch upon is to enjoy, celebrate & savour all our success, however small or big they might be. So if you hit that weekly goal, celebrate it! If you travel to a continent or country and that was your medium- term goal, take time to sit back and savour it!

Success is meant to be celebrated and not something that keeps you in the shadows, constantly wanting more, which is often the case with monetary success. It's an endless loop of wanting more and more and never being happy or satisfied.

We're all successful in something or the other and every human being on this Earth has something to aspire to.

So it's important to define our success with a clear mind & heart and make sure that it aligns with our passions, interests & desires & most importantly our authentic selves, which can be in the near-term, medium-term or long-term.

And of course, order some cake and bake some cookies and round up your loved ones and enjoy all your success, weekly, monthly, yearly or quarterly.

Mindset Is Everything

"Whether you think you can, or you think you can't – you're right,"
- Henry Ford

Picture this: you're an outfield player in a football(soccer) team. Your team just concedes the second goal of the game, and there are 5 minutes left on the clock. How are you going to react? Are you going to play to your best abilities & rally your team to overturn the deficit of two goals by scoring three goals and win or equalise by scoring two goals and level the game, taking it to extra time? Or are you going to buckle and give up saying that it's not possible? It's 5 minutes plus added time, until the full-time whistle, do you think you can do it or not?

If your head says yes — That's an elite & a winning mindset. And mindset is everything. A game similar to this example I've stated actually happened to me in a competitive football match in my first year of college. I was on the football team playing as an attacking midfielder or number 10 (a position on the football pitch), we conceded a goal with five minutes left on the clock and we were all dejected but our captain 'P' issued a rallying cry from defense urging us to keep pushing & especially us in attack to overturn the deficit. I was eighteen but I was pumped & decided to push harder to score & turn the tides of the game. We were all motivated & fired up by P's rallying cry. Just then the manager who was this final year senior made a substitution getting on a player 'S'.

After S came on, I found a pass to him in space & he took a shot from way out which threw the opposition keeper off & it went in. 1-1. We were all ecstatic then shortly after kickoff we probed & attacked more and in the final minutes of the game S went through one on one & scored another goal making it 2-1. It was the final of the cup & we won scoring two goals in the last five minutes. I'll never forget that game. And the reason we won was because we didn't give up despite conceding a goal with five minutes left. It was a lesson I learnt for the rest of my life.

Especially in sports, mindset plays a critical aspect in player and team performances. In football, all players usually have the same range of skills at par with each other bar about 5 to 10% who are simply gifted. But the more confident players end up doing better in games on a regular basis and having a winning mentality and serial winning mindset separates the average players from the elite winners.

A few football managers who typify an elite winning mindset are surely Sir Alex Ferguson, Carlo Ancelotti, Pep Guardiola, Jurgen Klopp and Jose Mourinho. The aforementioned names are serial winners, reflected in their win-to-loss ratio. Sure defeats happen and no manager can have a 100% record, but these managers in the modern era of football have had the least losses as compared to all other modern-day managers across the globe and the diverse football landscape. In essence, it's their mindset which enables such starkly impressive records.

Sir Alex Ferguson's Manchester United teams have been notoriously infamous for coming back in the dying minutes of games to win. Football fans platonically call it "Fergie Time".

There have been numerous instances when Sir Alex's teams have come back from the dead to win games and trophies. One prime example was their 1999 Champions League win over Bayern Munich, who were leading the game 1-0 until the last 3 minutes of the game before Sir Alex's Manchester United team scored two goals to clinch the trophy, Ferguson's first piece of European silverware. The triumph has been discussed as the stuff of legend since then, not just by Manchester United fans but football fans across the globe.

Football is full of remarkable comebacks. Ask any Liverpool fan about Istanbul and they'll tell you that it was the greatest night and comeback in the club's history. Liverpool were down 3-0 to AC Milan in the first half of the UEFA Champions League final in 2004-05 and then overturned the three goal deficit by equalising and scoring three goals in the second half only to take the game to penalties and eventually win. Chelsea's 2012 UEFA Champions League triumph is another; against Bayern Munich of Germany on their home turf at the Allianz Arena. A late goal by Didier

Drogba served as the equaliser, and Chelsea won the game & trophy on penalties with Drogba scoring the winning penalty. The stuff of legend!

A winning mindset is all about comebacks, and who doesn't love a good comeback?

A winning mentality & mindset is the will to win and succeed despite being down & out and under the cosh. In another football analogy, if you're tackled and hurt and injured suffering from cuts and gashes on your knees and bleeding, would you continue playing to win the game or would you say you can't play and walk off the pitch?

Personally, I've played through pain on numerous occasions on the football field. And top players have played through broken noses and after receiving stitches. A prime example is John Terry, former captain of Chelsea FC and one of the greatest defenders in the history of the Premier League, who exemplified playing through pain and injury & putting his body on the line for his club's badge. Even ice hockey legend Wayne Gretzky can vouch for playing with injury, as he did in the Stanley Cup.

A winning mentality is never giving up & always wanting to win and succeed.

Life is like a football pitch — Life is going to tackle you and bring you down, and there are times when you're going to be in pain and struggling, but how you react to it defines how your present & future, both immediate and long term, will be. You have to just get up from being tackled and keep chasing that goal. No incident or ordeal is permanent, life is transient, and how we react to our bad times, failures and mistakes, and what our mindset is like defines how our life will be.

So, cultivate a winning mindset at every instance of your life. Play to win, don't play to just make up the numbers. And always remember, if you're tackled or hurt by life, just get up & keep running…

Balance & Wu Wei – From Alan Watts to Ramana Maharshi & Stoicism

You've probably seen the scene from the movie *The Matrix* where Neo (Keanu Reeves) dodges bullets, by arching his body backwards. This comes after another character in the movie, Morpheus, trains Neo to "free his mind". This, in a way, can be likened to *Wu Wei*. There's something profoundly liberating in the notion of *Wu Wei*, a core tenet in Taoism that translates to "effortless action" or "doing without doing."

For Alan Watts, one of the great interpreters of Eastern philosophies, *Wu Wei* wasn't about passivity but the art of going with the flow; moving with the natural order of things rather than imposing our will upon them. Watts understood that in a world obsessed with productivity and control, *Wu Wei* suggests another way, i.e. a life led by intuition, trust in the unknown, and harmony in flow. Drawing from Lao Tzu's *Tao Te Ching*, Watts explained that *Wu Wei* is all about balance.

Imagine floating down a river. You could swim against the current, tire yourself out, or you could let the river guide you & flow along with it.

It's uncanny but you must've noticed how some ideas & things come about in life at their particular time just like the flow of a river taking turns as it does. That's *Wu Wei*—flowing with life rather than forcing it. Watts often pointed out how our constant need for productivity and "more" creates an imbalance that distances us from our essential selves. We're often so busy chasing outcomes, that we miss the simple, organic flow of life, and according to Watts, it's in letting go that we find ourselves again.

Watts also found echoes of this concept in Indian philosophy. Rabindranath Tagore, for example, wrote about the harmony found in slowing down, in observing the world instead of trying to usher a sense of control to it.

Jiddu Krishnamurti, too, advocated the freedom of the mind when it is not burdened by incessant thought and constant action. Tagore and Krishnamurti had their unique lenses to the philosophy of balance and letting go, but both resonated deeply with the essence of *Wu Wei*.

Tagore, in works like *Stray Birds* and *Fireflies*, often explored the theme of living harmoniously with the world, believing true freedom and creativity thrive when we are in sync with the rhythms of nature. His poetry encourages readers to pause, observe, and experience life without rushing, underpinning the value of balance in *Wu Wei*.

Krishnamurti's teachings meanwhile, align closely with this perspective but go further into the mechanics of thought and awareness. He believed that true peace arises when the mind isn't driven by the incessant need for achievement or validation but instead rests in the present; its natural state of peace.

According to Krishnamurti, insight and wisdom come about not from forcing answers or reaching for goals but from a quiet, mindful observation of life, and by seeing things as they are without attachment or aversion & flowing with the balance of the natural flow.

These perspectives on *Wu Wei* & flow can also be found in the teachings of Ramana Maharshi. For those who don't know about him, Maharshi was an influential Indian sage and spiritual teacher known for his teachings on *self- inquiry* and *non-dual awareness* called *advaita vedanta*. Born in 1879 in Tamil Nadu, he underwent a profound spiritual awakening at the age of 16, which led him to seek refuge at the holy mountain Arunachala. Maharshi's central teaching was the method of *atma vichara*, or "self-inquiry".

The West, has for centuries, tried to understand and decode consciousness, which is explained in texts like the *Rig Veda*, and Western thinkers have tried explain it scientifically, often called 'the hard problem', but I'd like to think of it as a collective consciousness. A consciousness that is experienced personally by every one of us individually and collectively. It's like a giant tree of flowing consciousness with each one of us being its separate branches and leaves, living and growing, part of something greater but experiencing it in a personal way. But what is the 'giant tree'? Thinkers & sages like Sri Aurobindo call it the "supra-mental", "higher collective consciousness", or the "higher self", a higher understanding which they attribute to being what the source of the giant tree is. But that topic is for another discussion and perhaps another book!

Maharshi's philosophy of self-inquiry & surrender is similar & blurs into congruence with the Taoist concept of *Wu Wei*, or "effortless action." Both perspectives suggest that aligning with a deeper, unforced flow of existence is the key to an aligned, peaceful, and meaningful existence.

Maharshi's teachings echo that true understanding and peace come from abiding in one's natural state of self-awareness, not by chasing or grasping at outcomes. He encouraged seekers to dissolve the ego-driven will, allowing life to unfold through us, rather than being pushed by us, mirroring *Wu Wei's* concept of quiet surrender.

There's this line from the movie *Life of Pi*, where the protagonist Pi suggests "I suppose in the end, the whole of life becomes an act of letting go…", which in essence, is the cornerstone of *Wu Wei* and Maharshi's teachings.

In *Wu Wei*, as in Maharshi's teachings, we are called to release the illusion of control. Maharshi suggested that real growth happens not through forced actions or relentless ambition, but by being present and rooted in stillness, where clarity and insight arise naturally. But the act of "letting go" and "surrender" to the higher calling or the higher consciousness, or simply the unknown Maharshi argues, is the path towards self-actualisation and the way forward for our own unique paths through life to unfold.

But we need to understand that for Watts, and indeed for many seekers of Eastern wisdom, the call of *Wu Wei* and Taoism isn't just about escaping work or abandoning effort. It's about remembering that true power comes not from force, but from attunement with the natural flow.

Balance isn't the absence of effort, but the presence of the mind to gracefully move with the flow. As Watts suggests, it isn't about not cutting wood, but cutting wood along the lines where it's most easy to be cut. Furthermore, Watts says, "Stop measuring days by degree of productivity and start experiencing them by degree of presence." And when we see life this way, every moment becomes an opportunity to practice *Wu Wei*, to find balance, and to connect with something larger than ourselves.

In essence, when it comes to our work & professional life, it's about **eradicating the outcome & focussing on our effort** being fully present. When we **eradicate** our wants & **the outcome** of our work we can flow seamlessly while putting in effort that merges with the 'flow state' of *Mushin* (which I will explore in a later chapter). It's paramount to let go of our wants & the outcome & just wholly focus on the work at hand & not push too hard but flow with it.

Instead of wanting & asking for things to yourself in thought, prayer or self-dialogue, focus solely on putting in the effort & leave the outcome to the natural flow & order of the universe. This is a concept that has helped me profoundly. To just focus on the work & the effort of your goals & targets in your best capacity & leave the outcome to the universe or the unknown, by trusting in it. It's an act of trust & faith in the universe, or a higher consciousness or just **faith in the unknown.**

It's just like setting a travel destination & trusting the travelling experience to unfold in its own beautiful way.

It's a conscious act of **'letting go' of the outcome** or result & **focusing solely on your effort & work**, i.e. the **things you can control**, and if a certain outcome results in a door closing, trust that it's not the path for you while on the other hand, if some results pan out favourably, they could be the exact path you need. It's about letting go of the *result* & focusing on the *process*.

This is concept is also echoed in Stoic philosophy. The Stoic philosophy of control is best summarised by Epictetus in *The Enchiridion* where he writes, "Some things are up to us, and some things are not up to us." So this fundamental idea suggests that we as individuals should focus our energy only on what we can influence such as our thoughts, actions, and reactions while accepting with equanimity that what lies beyond our control, like external events, people's opinions, or fortune is an act of embracing of the unknown.

This philosophy is closely related to the *Dichotomy of Control*, a key Stoic principle that teaches resilience and inner peace by directing effort toward personal virtue rather than external outcomes. A practical example is found in Marcus Aurelius' *Meditations*, where he reminds himself that while he cannot control others' actions, he can control his response: "You have power over your mind—not outside events. Realise this, and you will find strength," he wrote.

This Stoic principle teaches that peace, resilience and progress come from focusing only on **what we can control** and **letting go of what we cannot.** Our thoughts, actions, and attitudes are within our power, but external events like results, outcomes, other people's opinions, unexpected setbacks, or global circumstances are beyond it. By directing energy toward self-improvement and rational decision-making instead of worrying about uncontrollable factors, we're more attuned with balance & *Wu Wei*.

Together, all these concepts & prominent thinkers expand the concept of *Wu Wei*, suggesting that real clarity and fulfilment comes when we free ourselves from the demands of society & our own demands for constant productivity & the results we want & take the path of *natural flow*. They invite us to embrace simplicity, finding meaning in everyday moments and trusting that the most profound realisations often arrive in the *pause* rather than in the *push*.

All the perspectives mentioned in this chapter converge on one principle i.e. that life's beauty is in its balance & harmony with the natural flow just as *Wu Wei* teaches.

Eckhart Tolle on Living in The Moment & Jiddu Krishnamurti on Fear

"Live in the moment," is a phrase you have probably heard a lot, but what does it really mean? The essence of living in the 'now' is more than just a simple mantra. Rather than just an ideal, it's a transformative way of 'being' that shifts how we experience life itself. This concept is deeply explored in Eckhart Tolle's book *The Power of Now* and is central to Zen Buddhist teachings. They both elucidate the importance of fully embracing the present moment, and how doing so can unlock peace, clarity, and freedom from suffering.

In *The Power of Now*, Tolle explains that most of our mental and emotional suffering comes from living in the past or projecting our minds into the future. We often replay past mistakes, regrets, or trauma in our minds, allowing them to invade our present. At the same time, we tend to worry about the future— things like, what might happen, what could go wrong, what we need to achieve, that risk we are scared of taking, or how that opportunity or decision could turn out & so on.

Zen Buddhism calls this *the illusion of time*. In reality, the past is gone, and the future hasn't yet arrived. The only true reality we have is the present moment. By dwelling on what has already happened or anxiously anticipating what could come, we miss out on the serenity & peace of *now*. In essence, it's the only place where life actually unfolds.

The teachings in Zen Buddhism encourage a deep mindfulness of the present. When you are fully engaged in what is happening *right now*, you connect with life on a profound level. There is no room for regret or worry seeping in because the mind is completely focused on the present, where peace resides.

Tolle introduces the idea of the "pain body", which is an accumulation of past emotional pain that we carry with us like excess baggage. This pain body is triggered by negative thoughts and experiences, causing us to react emotionally to situations that remind us of past hurt. Living in the *now* is one of the most effective ways to transcend this pain, Tolle suggests.

When you are fully present, your attention is no longer consumed by the memories and emotional weight of the past. Zen teachings similarly encourage practitioners to not become entangled in their thoughts or emotions but to observe them without attachment & let them flow.

By practising this mindfulness of focussing on the present, you can experience life without the emotional baggage that often distorts our view of reality. Just like *the still water parable*, which I will explore in another chapter, your mind will return back to its normal state of peace, so it's just about focusing on the present moment when your mind begins to drift into the past or future.

The word 'mindfulness' has been thrown around a lot in pop culture but Zen Buddhism places great importance on mindfulness i.e. being fully aware and present in each moment. Whether it's drinking tea, walking, or even breathing, every activity is a form of meditation when done with full attention. This practice aligns with Tolle's advice to break free from the mind's constant chatter and to focus on the present, no matter how simple or mundane the task at hand might seem.

When you bring your awareness fully into the now, even the most routine actions become imbued with a sense of peace and clarity. You're no longer rushing to get through the task or distracted by thoughts of the future. Instead, you are *alive & in the moment*, connected to the present, and in turn, life itself.

Zen Buddhism further explores living in harmony with the natural flow of life. It teaches that resistance to what is, like whether through wanting to change the past or control the future, only leads to suffering.

This surrender doesn't mean passivity. We need to actively engage with the present moment, fully and without distraction, trusting that the present contains everything we need. In this state of presence, creativity, joy, and peace naturally arise.

Jiddu Krishnamurti, one of the great spiritual teachers of the 20th century, offered profound insights into the nature of fear (which stems from thoughts about the past or future). Krishnamurti argues that fear is often more about anticipation than reality, a product of the mind clinging to imagined future outcomes or past trauma or pain or suffering. But his most striking perspective is that fear, at its core, is nothing more than a sensation; one that dissipates when we are fully aware of it.

Krishnamurti encourages us to see fear as merely a sensation that arises in the body and the mind. He suggests that fear often arises as a result of the thoughts we attach to it, but in itself, it is a fleeting experience or bodily sensation.

Krishnamurti teaches that if we can observe this sensation of fear without immediately reacting to it, without trying to push it away or suppress it, or attaching thoughts to it, we begin to see it for what it is: a transient sensation. He says, "Fear only exists when we are not paying attention to it. The moment we are fully aware of fear, it begins to lose its power over us."

The key, Krishnamurti suggests, is not to resist or escape fear, but to be fully aware of it in the present moment. By doing so, we strip away the layers of thought and anticipation that often amplify fear into something overwhelming. Instead, we experience it in its raw form, just a sensation, like a breeze passing through the body.

This idea mirrors the teachings of *The Power of Now* and Zen Buddhism. When we remain fully present with fear, without judging or analysing it, we stop feeding it with our thoughts. It's the 'thoughts' we attach to the sensation of fear which makes it worse, but by itself, it's just a bodily sensation. Zen teachings encourage us to see emotions like fear as clouds passing through the sky of our mind. They come and go, but the sky—the clear, peaceful awareness of the present moment & our mind's natural state—remains unchanged again.

Krishnamurti believed that true freedom comes from understanding the nature of fear and dissolving it through awareness. "To live without fear is to live in a state of complete freedom," he urged. This freedom isn't something we achieve through effort or control, but by allowing ourselves to be fully present with whatever sensations or emotions arise, without resistance. This practice of recognising fear as just a sensation and not attributing thoughts to it can help all those people who struggle with anxiety or pain from the past.

When we fully inhabit the present moment, as both Tolle and Krishnamurti emphasise & advocate, fear & suffering dissolve. You no longer see fear as something threatening or painful. Instead, you see it as a passing sensation, i.e. an experience to be observed, not dreaded.

It's easier said than done, but with practice, this shift in awareness brings an immense sense of peace & freedom.

You can skip to the chapter of Still Water: A Zen Parable for a practical way of letting go of fear and negative thoughts.

A Modern Take on Self-Inquiry & What Spirituality Is

"The way is within" — *Unknown*

Spirituality is commonly mistaken to be about God. The moment people use the term spirituality, most people think it's about God or religion and so on and so forth. However, spirituality, as the name suggests, has more to do with the *spirit* and *finding oneself.* We are spiritual beings, long before physical, carbon- based lifeforms from celestial beginnings, if you study the cosmos and cosmology.

Eastern philosophy explicitly explores spirituality as the way to find the self and understand who you are. Self-inquiry and questioning the self are perhaps the best ways to understand more about the person you are and your innate make up. However, what I will suggest here in this chapter isn't about *self- actualisation*, which is the ultimate goal of self-inquiry, it's more practical and more of a modern take to understand your path and purpose, and to set you on your way to find things that are meaningful to you, despite Camus' Absurdism, I might add.

The year was 2016, and I had just come out of a business and financial debacle. My first business in my mid-twenties had failed spectacularly. While all my friends and peers were travelling all over the world, partying and attending gigs, hanging out and just enjoying post-undergrad working life and preparing for their Master's degrees, I had the brilliant idea to start a business, because, at the time, I thought that becoming monetarily successful in my twenties would let me enjoy life later on.

Not the worst notion and goal, but poorly executed and unaligned with my purpose.

I put in all my savings that I had made over the course of the previous four years doing sales and marketing jobs & started a broking firm.

Primarily stock broking, and also real estate broking. I studied finance and investing, I invested in a posh office and staff and spent all the money for franchise fees and office computers and began working at it.

I gave it two years from 2014 to 2016 but I couldn't get enough clients on the stock broking front, and enough to turn a profit on the real estate front.

In the end, I couldn't break even after two years and lost the bulk of my savings at the time, which was all I had made. But I learned valuable lessons in business & life.

I began mid 2016 almost broke and with no clue of what was ahead of me. That's when I began reading, writing, & journaling. I began reading about Buddhism and Buddhist teachings, this was after studying them all the way back in school, and I stumbled upon some books & talks by Wayne Dyer, Jiddu Krishnamurti and Ramana Maharshi, Rabindranath Tagore, Eckhart Tolle and Alan Watts who were proponents of Eastern philosophy and began reading Western philosophy from the likes of Nietzsche, Immanuel Kant, Plato, Da Vinci, and others while also constantly exploring sharing new music after creating a YouTube music channel.

It was then that I also fortunately got a job as a football journalist at a reputed upcoming sports content platform. That's about when I began to practice my own way of self-inquiry which most Eastern philosophy advocated.

The question I kept asking myself was, *"What do I really want?"*

And this process took a few months, I kept asking myself that question repeatedly and writing about what I would want as my ideal life, initially I got the usual answers — money, fame, power, stuff like that, but as I delved deeper and deeper and kept asking myself that question for months on end, and writing and journaling, I began to get the answers and discovered that my core passions were in writing, music, film, and football and combinations of them. I also figured out that I wanted to travel as much as possible & also that I wanted peace of mind & that I was most peaceful by the ocean and that I wanted to own a beach house and a beachside cafe some day.

That was what I truly wanted. Not the superficial stuff that my mind was throwing at me on the surface, but it came from the very essence of my being. And it all began to make sense and fall into place.

I began learning musical instruments and exploring musical avenues, I grew my YouTube music channel and sold it, I continued writing about football, a sport I had played since the age of nine, and had vast knowledge and expertise of and that I watched religiously throughout my life, and I began to write poetry as a way of expressing myself.

All this came from that period of contemplation and self-inquiry that lasted a few months, where I repeatedly asked myself the question "what do I really want?".

Fast forward to 2024, as I write this book and I've become an upcoming musician, producer, film composer and DJ and have spent 9+ years as a football, film & music journalist that has seen me transition to starting my own blogs. I'm learning programming to create music software, building upon my undergrad college education and I've written and published over 2500+ articles as a writer/journalist garnering over 4.5million reads and published my first poetry book called *The Indian Night* in 2022 and *Interludes to The Indian Buddha* in 2023. I also regularly write about various topics of my interest online and offer the world my perspective, as Kant suggested(which I will touch upon in another section).

Truth be told, I'm happy and perfectly aligned with my purpose — writing, music, film & football — and whether I make it big and become monetarily successful or not, I am living out what I really want to do. And that was only possible through self-inquiry.

Self-inquiry, in this sense, can point you towards your purpose and helps align yourself with the activities and work that's meaningful to you and where you can contribute with your skills and perspective. It's a method of delving deeper into your innate make up, and a way of finding the areas of interest and goals that resound naturally with you.

It also helps in learning what you truly want and yearn for in life. Initially, you will get a lot of superficial stuff on the surface when you practice this form of self-inquiry but in time, the more you ask yourself the question and the more you write, journal and reflect on the answers you get from asking yourself "What do I really want?", you get a clearer picture in due time.

The way is within. So try it out yourself. Ask yourself repeatedly, "What do I really want?" & the answers will come in time.

Bukowski's Words on Passion

"Find what you love, and let it kill you"— Charles Bukowski

Building upon the previous sections, finding your purpose, what you really want and uncovering your passions, are an essential part of living a meaningful and purposeful existence. But as I've explored in the chapter on *Albert Camus & Absurdism*, it's an idea we attach to our lives to give it purpose & meaning although there's no grander meaning out there in the universe. However, as it turns out, finding purpose is not such a bad thing.

The renegade American poet and philosopher Charles Bukowski couldn't have put it better. Bukowski's life was marred with rejection and sadness, and he lived very much like an outcast, consuming copious amounts of alcohol, but he eventually found success and recognition in the latter years of his life & posthumously for his writing and live readings of his poetry.

In his poem, Bukowski says, *"Find what you love and let it kill you. Let it drain you of your all. Let it cling onto your back and weigh you down into eventual nothingness. Let it kill you and let it devour your remains. For all things will kill you, both slowly and fastly, but it's much better to be killed by a lover..."*

There was an Instagram post I stumbled upon which suggested: "Try everything in your twenties, find what you love in your thirties, find ways of making what you love pay you in your forties, and try not to work too much in your fifties, and ensure that you have lived and loved to the fullest and have no regrets about your life in your sixties and onwards".

A lot of times, people often call your passions, personal endeavours and projects irrelevant and "passion projects" or "hobbies" and that you have to be realistic and make a living doing your usual nine to five and so on.

But if you follow your passions & work at what you love doing the most and can make your passions translate to monetary pay that's the most fulfilling thing.

Your passions are ingrained into your very being and are very much part of who you are and what you can offer to the world. They are no accident, and are not random things you like. More often than not, they're essential and a path to follow and pursue diligently.

As I've mentioned earlier, I discovered my passions in writing, music, film and football. And have been able to grow my knowledge of those areas of interest and improve my skills at them slowly but surely and translate that into pay.

It's subjective from person to person, and only you can find out what your passions truly are.

But once you find your passions, work becomes an *act of play*, as Chinese philosophy suggests, and you're naturally working on things you love, so there's no forcing things and work becomes light, easy and lovable.

I found out that I was a naturally very creative person (it has its drawbacks): but for example, the position I play on the football pitch is also that of a number 10 or trequarista and at times a number 8 as a regista, and those are primarily creative positions on the field. Trequartistas and registas are the creative midfield players on the football pitch and most of the playmaking happens through them.

So even my position on the pitch while playing football since my teenage years, pointed towards doing creative work as an adult. Now, I explore my creativity through music and writing, which are my outlets.

Sure, you'll have some non-creative days, and there is burnout and the need to take breaks, but I'm totally aligned with what I love doing the most and that has translated into parallel careers following my passions.

Another way of practically finding out what your passions are, is by the methods suggested in the previous chapter and another question, which is *"What would you choose to do, if you had all the resources and time?"*

That's a question that can get you started on discovering your passions. Just suppose you had all the resources and means to accomplish something and all the time to do it in, what would you naturally do if you were posed with that situation? The more you explore that question, and write and analyse what you truly want to do, you'll be on course to discovering your innate passions.

I had the chance to meet a motivational speaker named Janet Attwood, whom my father had organised an event for in a hotel called Sea Princess in Juhu, Mumbai. She's the author of the book *The Passion Test* which is a systematic way to find your passions.

At the time, I wasn't very attuned with myself and listed some stuff that wasn't aligned with my passions, but her test is pretty useful and accurate as a way of uncovering your passions. At the end of her talk, she came to me and said, "Gaurav, it's been lovely, remember when in doubt, choose in favour of your passions."

And that was the last thing she said to me and the last time I saw her. But that statement lingered on in my memory, "When in doubt, choose in favour of your passions". That's all you need really.

It could be anything for you. Travelling, cooking, film, art, business, leadership, teaching, coaching, photography, finance, deep sea diving, mountain climbing, sailing, driving, studying, research, the list is pretty much endless.

So yes, there are ways to uncover your passions, so it's essential to find what works for you and how you can uncover the things you're naturally passionate about and drawn towards.

Passions are your way of expressing yourself and adding that bit of personal flavour to what you can contribute to the world.

So yes, as Bukowski says, find what you love and let it be the end of you!

Make Room for Art in Your Life

"Art washes away from the soul the dust of everyday life"
— Pablo Picasso

i) **Art In Times of Crises**

Music and the arts have their own beautiful and pervading way of touching people's lives in a way no other man-made conception can. This is ever more prevalent in times of deep crises. In times of dire despair, in our darkest moments, the presence of art gives us a new breath of life, meaning, solace, strength, hope and that spark to help us carry on.

In his book, *Man's Search For Meaning* (1946), Viktor E. Frankl, a former holocaust survivor, described a '*cabaret*' that took place at the concentration camp he found himself in as follows:

"A hut was cleared temporarily, a few wooden benches were pushed or nailed together and a programme was drawn up. In the evening those who had fairly good positions in the camp — the Capos and the workers who did not have to leave camp on distant marches — assembled there. They came to have a few laughs or perhaps to cry a little; anyway, to forget. There were songs, poems, jokes, some with underlying satire regarding the camp. All were meant to help us forget, and they did help. The gatherings were so effective that a few ordinary prisoners went to see the cabaret in spite of their fatigue even though they missed their daily portion of food by going."

Frankl also notes that having some semblance of the arts and humour within the ghastly walls of the concentration camp was *"another of the soul's weapons in the fight for self-preservation"*

Similar to Frankl, another Jewish survivor of the holocaust, Otto Dov Kulka wrote vividly about the '*skits*' performed at Auschwitz. Born in Czechoslovakia in 1933, Kulka was sent to Theresienstadt and then to

Auschwitz when he was only a child. In his book *Landscapes of the Metropolis of Death* (2013), Kulka recalls how Herbert, a fellow inmate, made a lasting impression on him by exposing him to art in those dire times in the concentration camp:

"It was Herbert who gave me a copy of Dostoevsky's Crime and Punishment, Herbert who explained to me who Beethoven was, and Goethe, and Shakespeare, and about the culture they bequeathed us"

Kulka also tells of history lessons and artistic performances, including plays, concerts, and an opera for children organised by an inmate named Freddy Hirsch. Hirsch's barracks *'became the centre of the spiritual and cultural life of the place'* wrote Kulka. Gaining exposure to this diverse array & range of art forms made a telling mark on him for life, as he recounts that they *'unquestionably form the moral basis for my approach to culture, to life, almost to everything, as it took shape within me during those few months, at the age of 10 and 11'*.

Kulka also writes about another inmate of his name Imre, who organised a children's choir in the camp. Kulka reflects on the irony of how Imre's choice to teach the children in the camp a song about *'the brotherhood of man'*, trying to understand the *'terrible absurdity'* of playing the song *'opposite the crematoria of Auschwitz'*.

Music like Beethoven features in another holocaust survivor named Elie Wiesel in his book *Night* (1958). Wiesel was a teenager when he was sent from Romania to Auschwitz after being separated from his mother and sisters.

Wiesel witnessed the shocking brutality of the Nazis up close when he saw small children thrown into the flames and he recalls how something within him also died the night he witnessed it. He writes that his soul was *'invaded — and devoured — by a black flame'*.

Wiesel and his fellow inmates eventually reached the Gleiwitz camp, where they were forced to assemble into an already overpacked barrack where people were piling on top of each other and being trampled on and crushed to death. Wiesel writes about how a Jewish violinist named Juliek played Beethoven's concerto on his violin. He writes, *'that night in a dark* barrack where the dead were piled on top of the living', 'Never before,' 'had I heard such a beautiful sound.'

"The darkness enveloped us. All I could hear was the violin, and it was as if Juliek's soul had become his bow. He was playing his life. His whole being was gliding over the strings. His unfulfilled hope. His charred past, his extinguished future. He played that which he would never play again."

Juliek died the same night in that camp in what were his final hours on the violin and his final swan song.

A female holocaust survivor named Nelly S. Toll in her book *Behind the Secret Window: A Memoir of a Hidden Childhood During World War Two* (1993), writes about how she and her mother went into hiding in a small room in an apartment, and a neighbour bought her some paints. Painting became and outlet for Toll; a means of forgetting the war and something that offered solace during those turbulent times.

She writes: *"Once I started to paint, a new world opened up for me. It was as if the little box of watercolours made a bright path straight through the apartment walls to the outdoors ... In my pictures, there was no war, no danger, no police, and no tears."*

There's a common theme in all these accounts of these survivors of the holocaust. The recurring theme is that all of them turned to some form of art, either music, literature, writing, painting, education, or creativity in their darkest hours.

All these people describe in detail in their accounts of WWII about how art gave them hope, and strength and carried the light in the darkest periods of their lives.

ii) Art As A Means of Making Life Better & The Brain Healthier

"Go into the arts. I'm not kidding. The arts are not a way to make a living. They are a very human way of making life more bearable. Practicing an art, no matter how well or badly, is a way to make your soul grow, for heaven's sake. Sing in the shower. Dance to the radio. Tell stories. Write a poem to a friend, even a lousy poem. Do it as well as you possibly can. You will get an enormous reward. You will have created something." — Kurt Vonnegut.

As a musician and writer myself, I'm a huge advocate of the arts. Turning to the arts helped me reinvent myself and survive my most arduous moments. As I've elaborated in the earlier sub-section, art gives means of sustenance and the will to go on in our most darkest hours. However, in this sub-section, I look at how art washes away the mundane and breathes life into our moments.

The arts & humanities carry a special kind of weight in our lives and as one of the grandest forms of human expression, they bring moments to life and add colour to the otherwise mundane and dull situations of everyday life, helping us forget our pain, strife, and struggles. Music & the arts kindle in our hearts the flames of wonder and hope & hold their rightful place as a vital cog in the process of living and which make us live more enriched lives.

It's perhaps crucial to make room for art in your life. Whether that's music, film, painting & sketching or reading books and poetry, art becomes a way of living and offers solace & a distraction from the usual trials & tribulations or the blankness of everyday life.

Art can help you understand yourself and explore how you feel i.e. a deeper understanding of your emotions. Art also provides perspective and opens the mind to new ideas, stories, passions and experiences. Furthermore, art acts as a bridging mechanism that connects the inner workings of our minds, in thoughts and ideas, and bridges it with our perception and experiences.

There's a new field of research called neuroaesthetics; with the use of brain imaging and other techniques & technology of neuroscience, neuroaesthetics explores the relationship between art and the brain.

It examines how the brain processes and responds to art and the emotions these images and sounds evoke. The area of study explores the neurological processes and mechanisms that lie under our perception and appreciation of art.

It is a multidisciplinary field that combines neuroscience, psychology, and art theory to explore how art affects the brain. Neuroaesthetics research has helped to identify the cognitive processes involved in understanding and appreciating art, as well as the neurological and psychological mechanisms that underlie our appreciation for beauty.

With the help of neuroimaging technology, neuroscientists have discovered that there is an area of the brain called the medial orbital frontal cortex that always "lights up," or correlates with the perception of beauty, whether it is in response to visual, musical, mathematical, or even moral beauty. Although each type of experience activates different combinations of areas in the brain, the overlap always occurs in the medial orbital frontal cortex.

In their book *Your Brain on Art* neuroscientists Susan Magsamen and Ivy Ross offer a vision of what a life lived with an aesthetic mindset could look like.

Magsamen says, "Curiosity, surprise, wonder — all attributes found in art for the maker or the beholder — these are really important for human development. Researchers are finding that we as humans are hard-wired for aesthetic experiences. The arts are not just fundamental aspects of our humanity, but also essential to our well being."

She further adds, "We have 100 billion neurons, and the way we grow and learn is through neuroplasticity. The more enriched environments, the more sensorial — not chaotic, but in a way that feels safe and often novel — is how our brains grow dramatically." "Art can create new neuropathways in the brain because this happens through sensorial experience. With high visual stimulation, if we see a lot of art or make a lot of art, we are growing dramatically & feeding parts of our brain. And it's never too late to create an enriched environment, whether as the maker or the beholder in any art form."

Here are some ways Magsamen & Ross suggest to bring more art into your life:

- **Develop an arts practice:** Developing an arts practice like music, dancing, colouring, doodling, painting, photography, writing, sculpting or knitting, or any other art form can do wonders for your health and offers a creative outlet for your mind. "We hope that people start to think about 20 minutes of an arts practice, whatever that is, throughout the day," Magsamen says.

- **Appreciate art in your daily life:** It doesn't have to be an art workout — it can be an effort to appreciate the art in your daily activities. Appreciating art in your daily life is a great way to bring more creativity, joy, and beauty into your life. You can start by taking the time to look at art in its many forms, such as sculptures, paintings, photographs, and architecture. Notice the details, the colours, and the lines.

  Spend a few moments admiring the beauty of the artwork, and let yourself be inspired by it. If you don't have access to art galleries or museums, then take the time to appreciate the art in your home or the artwork of the people around you. Look for the beauty in your everyday life, such as the patterns of a flower, the colours of a sunset, or the sky and trees and the clouds. Appreciating art can give you a greater appreciation for the world around you and inspire you to find beauty in even the simplest of things.

- **Be creative about living with art:** Other ways to live with the arts include waking up to smells & observing surroundings and nature that make you happy. Small things like singing in the shower, gazing at the clouds and the sky & observing nature. Living with art is an excellent way to bring creativity and beauty into your home.

  You could start by exploring different art forms and finding pieces that speak to you. If you're looking for a more budget-friendly way to decorate, try creating your own pieces of art or finding unique objects that have special meaning to you.

  Display your artwork in unexpected places and use art, even posters, to create a unique atmosphere and add personality to your home. Consider creating a theme or colour palette that you can use throughout your home. Appreciating and creating art can help inspire new ideas and perspectives, so don't be afraid to experiment and be creative with your living space.

Make Your Own Waves

Apart from these points, there's also music, film & reading. So make some time for listening to music; it lights up several areas of your brain. You could start your own vinyl collection as well, but listen to music regularly, sometimes while working too so that it feels less of a burden to work while some music plays in the background. You could also sit by a fire, sip & eat something & listen to your favourite bands & artists. It can be extremely therapeutic & refreshing.

Make it a point to watch at least one film a week. This practice can help you recharge & refresh yourself. I usually try to watch at least 1-2 films every week, especially when I feel like there's nothing to do. If I'm a bit fatigued or don't feel like picking up my instruments or writing, watching a movie helps refresh my perspective.

Pay close attention to the plot, the dialogue, the visuals, the score, and the cinematography, and maybe write about them in your journal or like I do, I log on to Letterboxd (a film social network) & add an entry & review into my film diary after watching & analysing a movie. This art appreciation helps strengthen the brain. And of course if there's a movie you want to catch in the theatre, go ahead & book your tickets.

Read your favourite books in a comfortable setting. Just like films, reading transports you into a world of their own. Find a cozy spot & read, read, read.

It's Never Too Late to Start

"Sometimes too late is just in time." — C.J. Carlyon

It's never too late to start something new or to start doing the things you love. That's the beauty of life, we can start fresh whenever we want, except we tell ourselves we can't because of excuses like age, wealth, status, education, or whatever your excuse might be.

Ageing is inevitable and at the end of the road, would you want to look back and reflect on your life and regret that you never started or began doing the things you loved and wanted to do the most?

The time to act is now. Not later, not because of some excuse, the time is now!

Whatever you've been putting off for whatever reason, it's never too late to begin and become a master in that particular skill or endeavour.

As a child, I always loved music and would record songs off the radio onto tapes and music was a huge part of my childhood. I wanted to learn to play the bass guitar when I was in school; this was when I was in my teens. I wanted to learn bass and start a band. However, my parents told me that it would interfere with my studies — a typical Indian middle-class answer and notion.

As I grew older, I began to explore music further, mainly listening to and curating mixtapes and in school I would burn mp3 CDs and sell them to my schoolmates. In college, I was appointed as the in-house DJ at the most frequented pub in the township of Manipal, where I did my Bachelor's degree in Engineering at MIT, Manipal (India's MIT). But coming back, it was the universe's way of pointing me & my life towards music (which I'll come to in the chapter 'Connecting The Dots - The Steve Jobs Perspective').

It was clear that I loved music. And it was clear that music was my path for the future. After several years of working various jobs, a failed business venture, and losing all my accumulated savings, I finally got a steady job as a football journalist and so with the salary that I received, I bought two guitars and piano at 27 and began my journey learning & spending time learning them.

My acoustic guitar, an Ashton D20 BK, I named Magdalena of Australian make, my electric guitar a Fender Squire Bullet Stratocaster I named Audrey, manufactured in Indonesia & my electric Yamaha piano Winona, from China, became my closest friends.

Taking this leap into the process of learning instruments came at 27, a little over a decade after my wish to learn bass and it was liberating and pivotal. Until then, I kept telling myself I was too old to learn musical instruments and that I missed the bus, and kept putting it off, but I eventually found a way to learn & spend time learning instruments and it was by far one of the greatest decisions I made.

I decided that I didn't want to look back on my life in my 50s and 60s and regret not taking up learning musical instruments, so I just took the decision and acted immediately, figuring out the eventual outcome later.

And now several years on, I'm an intermediate guitarist, piano player and composer. Yes, the learning curve was steep and difficult, and yes, it was a tough and cumbersome route and journey, but with practice, work, dedication and just my love for music, which drove me onwards, I progressed considerably & the journey has been so satisfying.

The lesson is that, it's never too late to start doing the things you love or to start something new.

Stories about celebrities & masters of their fields i.e. people who started doing what they loved late on in their lives, are pretty well documented.

Harrison Ford, Samuel L. Jackson, and Morgan Freeman, to name a few, started their acting careers pretty late on — Harrison Ford was a carpenter until his mid-thirties and his break in the films *Star Wars* and *Indiana Jones*.

There are a host of examples of such stories online, these random grannies & grandpas picking up learning the guitar or piano & posting it online; turns out it's a great tonic as you age as well. If you think you can't do it now or think that you are too old or whatever your counterproductive reasoning is, I firmly suggest that you just take the leap and work at it, and worry about the outcome later.

Suppose you fail at succeeding in whatever facet or aspect of life you want to start anew and afresh, you'd at least have the experience and the fact that you gave it a shot, and not regret it later on in your life.

So, whether it's a new job, a business, a passion, a hobby, a skill, a travel plan, a relationship, or something that's totally different from your current expertise, and experience, just give it a shot! What's the worst thing that could happen?

You could lose some money, you could fail, you could get rejected, but at least you'd have tried and done what you wanted to do!

It's an act of faith, and trusting that doing what you love or embarking on a new project will eventually reap dividends. And more often than not, it's a great decision.

So go ahead and do it!

How To Make Hard Choices

"Nothing is more difficult, and therefore more precious, than to be able to decide" — *Napoleon Bonaparte*

Every day, we're faced with choices—small ones like what to wear, what to eat, which route to take to work, and others. But at different points in life, we come across bigger, more challenging decisions, the ones we feel could really change our lives, for better or worse.

These harder choices can be about what career to choose, where to live, whether to move to a different city or country, who to marry and other tough calls.

When we compare easy choices to hard ones—an easy choice usually has one option that clearly stands out as better. In a hard choice, both options have their own rewards, but also their own drawbacks and are at par.

Because both options might seem better or worse in some ways, we end up thinking about them over and over, trying to figure out which is the best. This happens because, in tough choices, both options often seem equally good, with neither being outrightly better.

Ruth Chang experienced this dilemma after finishing university. She had to choose between becoming a full-time philosopher or a lawyer. As most people would in this situation, she went with the safer option and chose law. But after some time as a lawyer, she realised it wasn't the right fit for her. Eventually, she returned to her passion—philosophy.

"Fear of being an unemployed philosopher led me to become a lawyer, and as I discovered, lawyering didn't quite fit. It wasn't who I was. So now I'm a philosopher, and I study hard choices, and I can tell you, that fear of the unknown, while a common motivational default in dealing with hard choices rests on a misconception of them."

"It's a mistake to think that in hard choices, one alternative really is better than the other, but we're too stupid to know which, and since we don't know which, we might as well take the least risky option."

"Even taking two alternatives side by side with full information, a choice can still be hard. Hard choices are hard not because of us or our ignorance; they're hard because there is no best option,"

"Now, if there's no best option, if the scales don't tip in favour of one alternative over another, then surely the alternatives must be equally good… But that can't be right." says Chang in her TED Talk.

Now, think about a choice between a job you love and one that pays more—a common hard decision many of us face.

So, what do we do?

You're thinking it over, and then suddenly, the higher-paying job offers an extra $500 or $1000 a month. What would you do?

Most people would go for the higher pay. But if both choices seemed equally good to you at first, the extra cash might make the higher-paying job seem like the better option now.

Chang uses another example—choosing between a career in graphic design or becoming an investment banker. The graphic design role could offer more time with family, more passion for the work, and a better work-life balance. On the other hand, the investment banking job comes with more money and faster career growth.

Both seem like good choices, but throw in an extra $500 or $1000 on the banking job side, and suddenly, it tips the balance.

Most people would choose the banking job and enjoy the money for a while, but might later regret not following their passion later.

Chang argues that, as creatures of the post-Enlightenment era, we often believe that scientific reasoning is the best way to make decisions. But that's not always true.

In science, comparing two numbers gives you three possibilities—one is bigger, smaller, or equal to the other. But when we try to apply this logic to life choices, we make a mistake by trying to approach them too logically.

These decisions go beyond science and logic. They are human. They're about what it means to live and experience life.

The answer lies in introspection and shifting our perspective. Instead of focusing on external factors like what we'll get out of each choice, we need to look inward and base the decision on who we are, and what aligns with us as people.

This could be our passions, our goals, what we want from life, what's best for our family in the long run—basically, what matters to us.

Maybe, we need to start appreciating these hard choices for what they are—a key part of living as conscious human beings.

This shift in perspective can move us from stressing and overthinking to feeling calmer and choosing what fits with our core values. Sure, the passion-driven job might give you more meaning, flexibility, and time with family, but the higher-paying job could make you and your loved ones financially secure.

Imagine a world where you always made the best, most optimised choice. Every decision, every moment of your life, was perfectly calculated. It would feel like you were living in a video game, where every move is predetermined, and you always take the "right" turn—like a version of Super Mario that always eats the mushrooms and never misses a step.

"It's here, in the space of hard choices, that we get to exercise our normative power — the power to create reasons for yourself, to make yourself into the kind of person for whom country living is preferable to the urban life. When we choose between options that are on a par, we can do something really rather remarkable. We can put our very selves behind an option."

"Here's where I stand. Here's who I am, I am for banking. I am for chocolate doughnuts. This response to hard choices is a rational response, but it's not dictated by reasons **given to us**. Rather, it's supported by reasons **created by us**."

"When we create reasons for ourselves to become this kind of person rather than that, we wholeheartedly become the people that we are. You might say that we become the authors of our own lives."

"So when we face hard choices, we shouldn't beat our head against a wall trying to figure out which alternative is better. There is no best alternative. Instead of looking for reasons out there, we should be looking for reasons in here: Who am I to be?," argues Chang in her TED Talk.

Maybe the hard choice you're facing isn't as bad as it seems. Instead of looking for external reasons or fearing the outcome, look inside. And instead of dreading tough decisions, try to embrace them. Remember, nothing is ever final and you can always choose differently later.

In the end, the choices we make, especially the tough ones, are part of life. They shape who we are. So, instead of worrying about making the "right" decision, maybe we should just choose what feels true to us.

This Is Water —David Foster Wallace's Message

"This isn't really about the capacity to think, but rather about the choice of what to think about." — David Foster Wallace

David Foster Wallace was an American author and essayist, best known for his novel *Infinite Jest*. His 2005 commencement speech, *This Is Water*, delivered at Kenyon College, became iconic & revelatory for its deep insights into everyday awareness. Wallace stressed upon the value of choosing how to think, urging graduates to resist default modes of selfishness and cynicism in their world view & everyday living experience.

In his speech, he encouraged empathy, and consciously shaping one's worldview to avoid being trapped in habitual thinking, often likened to swimming in "water" without realising what the 'water' is. The speech became a philosophical reflection on the power of perspective, which I will summarise in this chapter.

In his speech *This Is Water,* David Foster Wallace urges the power of **awareness** and **choice** in everyday life. He explores the human tendency to operate on autopilot, to default to a self-centred perspective, where we unconsciously prioritise our own needs and experiences over those of others; where we are at the centre of the universe.

He provides the example of an everyday scenario, of going grocery shopping after a long day of work to illustrate how we interpret our frustrations in ways that reinforce this self-centred view. Our default setting makes us see the world through the lens of personal importance, leading us to feel irritated or even victimised by mundane inconveniences like grocery shopping.

But Wallace's central message is that this default perspective is not the only option. Through conscious effort, we can choose **how we interpret our experiences**. This is the real value of education, he says: "learning how to think, and more importantly, learning what to think about." Wallace challenges us to see beyond the default perspective, to become aware of the water we swim in i.e. our ingrained perspectives, and to consciously shift to a more compassionate, empathetic way of seeing the world.

In his words, the most important reality is that which is hardest to see, which is our own deeply ingrained default settings that shape how we perceive the world.

At the heart of *This Is Water* is the notion that the banalities of everyday life like standing in long lines, sitting in traffic, and dealing with tiny frustrations are what define much of our existence. It's easy to fall into patterns of frustration, feeling as if these moments are a personal inconvenience. However, Wallace argues that the ability **to perceive these moments differently** is a kind of liberation.

So, instead of seeing ourselves as the center of the universe, we can choose to step outside of this default setting realising that every person around us is living their own complex life, with their own struggles and frustrations, just like ours. This shift in perspective can transform the mundane into something more meaningful.

Wallace's analogy of the fish not recognising the water they swim in speaks to how we often fail to recognise the reality that shapes our lives. Just as the fish are unaware of the water surrounding them, we are often oblivious to the mental and emotional environments we create through our habitual thinking. It is only when we become conscious & aware of this "water", i.e. the everyday realities that surround us and our default mindset, that we can begin to live intentionally.

The real challenge, as Wallace suggests, lies in consistently choosing to be aware. This awareness, just like Tolle & Krishnamurti suggest, is this effort to consciously choose our perceptions, and is the solution to the banality of routine and the misery of being consumed by trivial frustrations.

The **freedom to choose what to focus our minds on**, Wallace argues, is the true definition of freedom. It allows us to see people and situations not as obstacles or annoyances, but as part of a shared human experience. Instead of assuming that the people around us are deliberately being difficult, we can choose to see them as individuals dealing with their own struggles & their fair share of life's hurdles.

Wallace insists that this awareness is key to living a compassionate and meaningful life, as it helps us break free from the prison of our own self-centeredness.

The speech ultimately reminds us that life is full of small, repetitive & oftentimes frustrating and perhaps mundane moments, and it's in these moments that our real life unfolds.

The wisdom of Wallace's words lies in recognising **that true power comes from being aware of our automatic thoughts and choosing to respond differently, i.e.** to see life in a way that fosters connection, understanding, and empathy. By stepping out of our default settings, we can transcend the banality of everyday existence and live with greater purpose.

In this sense, *This Is Water* aligns with philosophical ideas from various schools of thought, echoing teachings that remind us to wake up from the trenches of everyday life and recognise the deeper meaning shaping our actions.

David Foster Wallace's *This Is Water* can be seen as a bridge between Western and Eastern thought. In Western philosophy, Wallace's focus on choice and awareness aligns with existentialist ideas of personal responsibility in constructing meaning.

This Is Water also shares common ground with Eastern philosophies, particularly in its emphasis on awareness and mindfulness & a shift of perspective from the 'I'. Wallace highlights the importance of stepping outside the default, self-centred perspective, a concept closely aligned with the Buddhist notion of detachment from the ego & the illusion of the 'I'.

In Hinduism and Buddhism, the concept of awareness of the present moment & being present in the 'now', which I've explored in earlier chapters, echoes Wallace's idea of recognising "the water" we swim in. These are the unconscious thoughts, feelings & patterns that shape our lives, calling for a more deliberate & mindful way of observing these default thought patterns & interpretations & in turn our shared experience of life with others.

In essence, we must recognise 'the water'. We must see that we're sharing this experience with everybody else & furthermore, return to the natural stillness of our minds (which I will cover in a forthcoming chapter) away from the chatter of our thoughts while dealing with the mundane, banal and disheartening experiences life throws at us.

'This is water', then, is at the heart of what it means to live by being more aware of it, i.e. every moment, everyone, everything & every thought being part of a larger shared experience as compared to just a personal one.

You can find David Foster Wallace's 'This Is Water' speech online on YouTube and elsewhere.

Everyone Is on A Different Journey, So Stop Comparing

"There's no right or wrong path, just your own." - Unknown

It's easy & commonplace to look outward for our next move, or our path in life. As social creatures, we often look outside at what other people are doing and try to find ways to do things similar to others & it comes as a result of comparing ourselves to others whether they're our family, friends, or acquaintances. This practice is severely flawed. The reason is that everyone you know is on their own unique path.

Comparing your path to someone else's doesn't work when the destinations, starting points, and routes are unique to each person.

Consider the story of two childhood friends, Varsha and Malvika. They grew up together, went to the same schools, and shared similar interests. After graduating college, Varsha landed a high-paying corporate job, while Malvika decided to travel and explore the world before figuring out her career path.

Varsha quickly climbed the corporate ladder, bought a house, and seemed to have her life perfectly put together. Malvika, on the other hand, took her time. She backpacked through several countries, did odd jobs, and didn't have much of a plan.

From the outside, Varsha appeared to be "ahead," living a life of stability and success. Malvika, meanwhile, looked like she was drifting without direction. But what if Malvika compared her journey to Varsha's? She might feel like she was falling behind, wasting time, or not living up to society's expectations.

However, what Malvika was gaining—experiences, personal growth, and a broadened perspective—was exactly what she needed at that point in her life. Varsha's path wasn't better or worse, it was simply *different*.

Now, let's fast forward a few years. Varsha, despite her success, started feeling unfulfilled in her corporate job. She realised that her passions lay elsewhere, and she made the difficult decision to leave her stable career to pursue something more meaningful to her—writing.

Meanwhile, Malvika found a career in social work, where her experiences traveling helped her connect with people from different cultures and backgrounds. Both women took different routes, but they each found purpose and happiness in their own way.

Comparing ourselves to others often blinds us to the fact that there isn't one "right" way to live. Your path may involve quick success or take longer to unfold. It may involve big risks or a slower, steadier pace. But it's your journey, and that's what matters.

Another example is in creative fields. Take writers, for instance. One author might publish their first bestselling novel at 25, while another might not get published until they're 50. J.K. Rowling didn't become a household name until her 30s, after facing multiple rejections. By contrast, someone like Christopher Paolini published his first book, *Eragon*, as a teenager. Does that make Rowling's journey less successful than Paolini's? Absolutely not. They each had different experiences that shaped their stories, and both ultimately found success in their own time.

Take Hans Zimmer as another example. Today, he's one of the most celebrated film composers in the world, known for scoring iconic films like *The Lion King*, *Inception*, *Batman: The Dark Knight*, *Dune* and *Interstellar*. But Zimmer didn't follow the traditional path of a film composer. In fact, he didn't have formal classical training like many other composers. Instead, he started out playing keyboards in a band and working with synthesizers in the early stages of his career.

For a long time, Zimmer wasn't considered a "serious" composer in the traditional sense. His peers in the film industry had classical backgrounds and years of formal education in composition. If Zimmer had compared himself to them, he might have doubted his abilities or felt like an outsider.

But instead of comparing himself to classically trained composers, Zimmer leaned into his unique approach. He fused electronic elements with orchestral music, using emerging music technology creating a groundbreaking sound that would later define modern film scores. By trusting his individual journey, he didn't just find success, rather, he redefined what film music could be.

Had Zimmer focused on how others in his field were doing things, he might have stifled his creativity. But by embracing his distinct path, he became a pioneer, showing that the key to success is often found in what makes you different, not what makes you the same.

Coming to the root of the problem with comparison is that it often leads to feelings of inadequacy. We see someone else doing well and think, "Why am I not there yet?" "Why am I not doing that?" But we forget that we don't have all the information.

You might see someone thriving in their career, but you don't see the late nights, the setbacks, or the self-doubt they faced to get there. And even if you did, their struggles and triumphs won't mirror yours because their life circumstances, desires, and goals are completely different.

A common scenario is when you see a peer on social media sharing pictures of their seemingly perfect life—vacations, promotions, relationships. It's easy to feel envious or like you're falling short. But what social media rarely shows are the behind-the-scenes struggles. The person with the dream job might be struggling with burnout. The couple posting vacation photos might be going through tough times behind the scenes. What we see is just a snapshot, not the whole story.

The key is to realise that your journey is uniquely yours. Just because someone else is at a certain place in their life doesn't mean you need to be there too.

Your timing is different, your lessons are different, and so is your destination. What works for someone else might not be right for you, and that's okay. The only person you should be comparing yourself to is *who you were yesterday*.

To truly stop comparing, you need to embrace your individuality. Take pride in your own progress, no matter how slow or unconventional it seems. Everyone is learning, growing, and evolving at their own pace. Remember, life is not a race. There's no timeline that dictates when you should hit certain milestones.

Conforming to what you see others doing is something that needs to change so that you stay true to yourself & your own path, and not somebody else's. If you find yourself stuck in the chasms of comparison, free yourself of it immediately by reminding yourself that your path is unique to you.

So, the next time you find yourself tempted to compare your life to someone else's, remind yourself: we're all on different journeys. What matters most is staying true to your path, no matter how winding or unexpected it may be. The only journey worth focusing on is your own.

Still Water – A Zen Parable on How to Achieve a Peaceful State of Mind

"Anxiety is thought without control, Flow is control without thought"
- James Clear

If you were given a bowl of dirty & murky water & were asked to make it clear, what would you do?

Most people would suggest filtering the water or boiling it or treating it with some chemicals so that the dirt is removed. However, if you let the dirty water sit for a certain period of time, all the dirt settles on its own. The water becomes clean & clear after a certain period of time & that's how our minds also work.

Like the bowl of dirty water, our minds will also eventually settle if we don't try to filter, react or boil it. "The natural state of water is clear, & the natural state of our minds is also clear", suggests Joseph Nguyen in his book *Don't Believe Everything You Think*.

Just like that bowl of dirty water, our minds can become cluttered and clouded with thoughts, worries, and stress. We often feel the need to "fix" this mental noise by overthinking or reacting or trying to forcefully make it subside. But just as the water naturally returns to clarity when left undisturbed, so does our mind.

Thinking is the root cause of all your suffering suggests Nguyen & he compares thinking to quicksand stating that the more you fight it & the more you try to suppress or eradicate it forcefully, the worse it gets.

The solution, he suggests, is simple but profound: *let go*. Allow your mind to settle naturally, and it will return to its peaceful, clear state without force.

This is easier said than done, but with deliberate practice, and just knowing that your mind's natural state is that of peace & clarity & that it will eventually return to that state irrespective of all the chatter & all the thoughts & worries can be amazingly liberating.

Key takeaways from this idea are:

- Don't react to or engage with every thought.
- The natural state of your mind is peaceful and clear.
- No matter how chaotic your thoughts are, your mind will always return to its natural calm.
- Like a river that encounters rocks, your mind may occasionally face obstacles, but it keeps flowing.

This back-and-forth between thinking and non-thinking is a natural part of being human. While we can't completely stop thinking, we can spend more time in moments of mental stillness, leading to a greater sense of peace, clarity and joy. Peace arises from knowing that beneath all the mental clutter, there is always a calm, non-thinking state available to us.

The Zen parable beautifully illustrates this concept. Just like how the dirt in the bowl of water settles over time, so too will the clutter in our minds if we simply *wait*. If we react to every thought, which is like trying to stop barking dogs, we only stir up more mental chaos. But if we choose patience and stillness, the mind will naturally clear itself, just as the water does.

Instead of fighting or forcefully trying to stop your negative or distracting thoughts, allow them to subside on their own.

Be calm, be patient, and remember that your mind's natural state is one of clarity and peace. Like still water, given enough time, your mind will settle, and everything will become clear once more. All you need to do is trust in this process and allow it to happen.

With conscious practice this can be immensely liberating and help you achieve and cultivate more sustained moments of having a peaceful state of mind and eradicate moments where your mind is overthinking. It takes a bit of time to master, but it is amazingly helpful especially if you find yourself struggling with incessant thoughts.

Remember to just *let go*, and *know* that your **natural state of mind is one of peace**, and you'll be halfway there on your 'quiet mind' expedition.

Learn The Lessons of The Past

"If you focus on the hurt(of the past), you will continue to suffer. If you focus on the lesson(of the past), you will continue to grow." - Buddha

We all have our share of pain from the past. The past is done and over with, so it's really immaterial & counterproductive to contemplate about the pain of the past.

However, this is easier said than done. Our mind wanders and drifts, and if there's pain attached to a past memory, it resurfaces unannounced and unplanned into the present.

According to Buddha's teachings, the past is only a lesson for us to learn. And whatever the past mistakes or suffering you've been through, it's paramount to learn the lesson from that incident and not think about the incident itself.

The past can be tragic, unforgiving and very overpowering at times, and our pains and fears and negative thoughts arise from attaching to a painful past memory or memories. If you've had a painful past, you're not alone, everybody has their share of painful memories.

But it's up to you to learn the lesson from it, whatever it might be. The past is for learning the lesson, and you then apply that lesson to the present so that it doesn't affect your future.

Life always goes on and we always live no matter what our past may be like; it's over and done with.

There are a few techniques you can use to understand and liberate yourself from negative thought cycles about the past.

1. **Reflect On & Learn The Lesson:** So, something bad happened. But what was the lesson? If you ran a red light and met with an accident, the lesson is to not ignore the red light henceforth.

Whatever your past may be, reflect on it, however painful it may be and understand why it happened and how to ensure it doesn't happen again. This is essential and you have to ensure that you don't repeat the same mistake again.

2. **Understand it:** It's important to understand why that particular event happened. What did you do wrong? What did someone else do to you that was wrong? Why did it happen? Whatever happened was because of a cause and effect. So find the cause and ensure that you don't repeat the same thing again so that the effect isn't going to repeat itself.

3. **Release it:** The past is a closed chapter. Whatever it is that happened to you, happened and now it's over. So the pain, anguish, guilt, fear, whatever you're facing because of your past, in the present, release it. Forgive yourself, forgive the people who wronged you, forgive the circumstance, forgive and release it from yourself. It's the past. Just let go. Release it.

4. **Reframe It Positively:** The past happened and it's over & done with. So you can always change the way you think about it and recollect it. If something bad happened, you can say "Ok, …. happened, but it made me stronger" or "That happened…. but it helped me grow" or "… it built my resilience" or "….it built my character". You can always rewrite how you think about the past in a positive way, however tragic it might be. You're the author of how you see your past and choosing to reframe it positively is another way to overcome the pain.

5. **Focus On The Present:** Buddhism teaches us to live in the moment i.e. to live completely in the present. And all our pain and suffering comes from either i) dwelling on the past or ii) fearing the future. So essentially, at the root of your suffering is because you're either thinking about the past or thinking about the future. There's no other reason for your suffering, anxiety, fear, pain etc. other than drifting off into the past or thinking about the future. The easiest way to focus your mind and focus it on the present is to "watch breath", as Buddhism teaches. Essentially, focus your mind on the present.

These are some ways in which you can learn and grow from your past, however painful it might be. So, use these simple techniques and liberate yourself from your past, and most importantly learn from it so that it doesn't happen again.

Nature Therapy

Spending time with nature is a perfect reset & serves as a way to relieve our stress & rebalance our minds & bodies. A study from Japan found that people who spent 30 minutes gazing at trees reported a noticeable drop in stress and anxiety. It's called *Shinrin-yoku* or "forest bathing,". Just sitting in nature, soaking in the greenery, can lower your cortisol levels and calm your racing mind.

But it's not just the Japanese who advocate this. Research from the University of Michigan shows that spending time in nature, whether it's a park, forest, or even a backyard, can improve memory and cognitive function. One of their studies revealed that participants who walked in a tree-filled area did 20% better on memory tests than those who strolled through city streets. It's apparent that nature hits the reset button on our brains, boosting creativity, focus, and even problem-solving skills.

One study from the University of Exeter found that people who spent just 15 minutes walking in a park or forest reported feeling calmer and less stressed compared to those walking in urban areas. Another study where people were asked to stare at nature—trees, grass, open sky—for 30 minutes, resulted in their stress hormones dropping significantly, and their anxiety almost went away entirely. If 30 minutes with trees can have that effect, a whole day outdoors & time spent in the midst of nature can clearly help in reducing the stress & anxiety levels we encounter from time to time.

Spending time with nature has been ingrained into human life since the dawn of time. Our ancestors didn't just observe nature from afar, they lived *in* it, side by side, in the wild. Cavemen slept under starlit skies, ancient nomads followed the rhythms of the land, & seasonal changes and early civilizations built their entire cities & lives around the natural world.

We've evolved alongside nature, and it's no wonder that stepping outside today, whether for a walk in the woods or just to feel the sun on your face, makes us feel connected to nature & in turn, ourselves. I often say that a good view can do wonders, which is why I make it a point to find and travel to places with some surreal views to take in, even when I'm writing & working or making music.

Fast forward to the 2020s, and the irony is that we spend more time connected to the Wi-Fi & our phones than to nature. But our bodies & our minds, still crave natural settings. A simple 30-minute stroll under the canopy of trees can do away with a lot of stress & can reset your body & mind, as explored at the beginning of this chapter. Modern life has become a barrage of notifications and never-ending work cycles, but nature remains a *reset button* waiting just outside your door.

You don't need a mountain trek to feel the benefits, even small doses of greenery, like sitting in a park or walking by a lake, can elevate your mood and lower cortisol levels. It's almost like nature whispers, "slow down, take a breather," and in those moments, you're more connected to the natural setting & yourself.

Making sure you include observing or spending time with nature in your daily routine can help you immensely, so you should ideally pencil in some 'nature time' into your daily schedule. While this might seem insignificant on the surface, it actually can do away with a lot of stress. If inculcated as a habit and part of a daily or weekly routine, it can lead to a much more healthier and balanced lifestyle, especially as the habit compounds over time.

So, if you're feeling stressed or overwhelmed with work maybe it's time to step outside, get a little lost, and recuperate in the process.

Travelling Is the Best Use of Time & Money

Travel isn't just about a vacation or an escape. Seeing the world, and the diverse cultural differences, languages, people, the streets & modern-day taverns that serve drink and food can provide great perspective & provide soul-fodder for the mind away from your usual perspectives, while broadening your horizons, no matter where you're from.

Travelling can feel like life's secret ingredient and it serves as a solution to the mundane, often acting as a remedy of routine. In Phil Knight's memoir *Shoe Dog*, he explores how the journey that eventually birthed *Nike*, started not with boardrooms or grand strategies, but with a backpack, a few bucks, and an open itinerary.

Phil Knight's journey from aspiring entrepreneur to the founder of Nike epitomises the transformative power of travel. In his book *Shoe Dog*, Knight recounts how his trip around the world in his early 20s was pivotal to the rest of his life.

He didn't just see new places; he gained fresh perspectives. His visit to Japan led him to discover Onitsuka Tiger, the brand that would eventually become Nike's first product line. He also carefully observed Japanese culture and the processes behind how they worked and created the Onitsuka Tiger line of shoes. Without the exposure and insight Knight gained from travelling, his vision for Nike might never have materialised. This included deciding to name his brand 'Nike', after visiting the temple of the Greek god *Nike* on his travels.

Knight's "crazy idea" was sparked while he was literally traversing across continents, with his perspectives shifting with each country he explored.

He was onto something many successful people recognise, that travel isn't just about vacationing or seeing new sights. It's the purest form of personal education. Knight's global expedition inspired him to think outside the box— about life, culture, and business—and ultimately gave birth to his eventual Nike empire. It's a testament to how valuable travel can be, beyond the monetary investment, which is in actuality, the best use of time & money.

The road has taught countless others, as well. Steve Jobs credited his visit to India as the moment that shaped his view of simplicity and minimalism, concepts later woven into Apple's design ethos. The trip brought clarity, introspection, and a fresh understanding of the world beyond Silicon Valley for Jobs.

In many ways, Jobs returned home more attuned to the complexity of life, yet laser-focused on stripping away distractions, much like the sleek design of the iPod & the first iPhone.

But travel isn't just to learn lessons in business, it's a more wholesome experience to reinvent yourself and something that's refreshing and serves as a reset and urges a rethink. Travel isn't about reaching a destination; it's a process, a beautiful process, that unravels the lessons hiding in plain sight.

Take Anthony Bourdain for example, whose travels were never just about food. His experiences around the world taught him that the real wealth lies in human connection, in the stories behind the meals and the people who prepare them.

Travel gave him a sense of humility, a deep understanding that no matter where you go, we're all sharing this big rock together.

So, why is travelling the best use of time and money? For starters, travel teaches you to adapt. And that adaptability is priceless. It shifts your thinking, pushing your boundaries beyond the familiar, and exposing you to things you wouldn't even know to look for. You come back a different person; more nuanced, more open-minded, more resourceful. For Knight, Jobs, and Bourdain, travel wasn't just leisure; it was an essential chapter in their story of life and success, moulding them in ways no classroom or conference room ever could.

When it comes to how you spend your hard-earned cash, travel might just be the best bang for your buck. Think about it—you're not just buying a plane ticket or a hotel stay; you're investing in memories, perspectives, and stories that will outlast any gadget or piece of furniture you could buy.

Travel isn't just a luxury; it's an education in disguise with exploration at the heart of it. Tony Wheeler, the co-founder of *Lonely Planet*, once said, "All you've got to do is decide to go, and the hardest part is over." It's no secret that experiences trump material possessions every time. Even Richard Branson has echoed this sentiment, often pointing out that spending on travel isn't about spending at all—it's about enriching your life, creating a catalogue of stories, and gaining fresh perspectives that can't be bought off a store shelf. So really, it's not about *affording to* travel; it's about affording *not* to.

Every trip you take is an investment in your story, a way to understand yourself and the world better. Whether it's wandering through crowded markets in Marrakesh, watching the sunrise over the Grand Canyon, the Northern Lights in Iceland or like in my hometown city of Mumbai watching the sunset over Marine Drive or perhaps on a beach in Goa or Gokarna.

Every experience rewires you just a little and resets your body and mind. You might have experienced that when you get back home after any travel expedition, you're more attuned with yourself and at peace. I like to call it *the post-travel effect*. No catchy names there and it follows the points mentioned in the chapter on *Nature Therapy* but unlike a new car or product you buy that depreciates the moment you start using it, the value of travel only grows over time. Plus, you're making memories & gaining experiences to look back on when you're older.

From ancient humans who followed herds in search of food to medieval explorers of old, travel has been embedded deeply into the human condition. Our ancestors' journeys weren't just physical; they represented an insatiable human desire to connect, to learn, and to broaden horizons. Travellers weren't just wanderers, rather they were seekers of knowledge, and explorers driven by an insatiable curiosity to explore the unknown.

From crossing deserts to navigating uncharted seas, their journeys reflect how deeply ingrained exploration is in our human makeup and psyche. Travel, even then, was about more than just survival; it was about discovery, expanding the human mind, and evolving our understanding of the world.

What makes travel so timeless is how it taps into this primal urge for discovery. In a way, to be human is to be restless, always searching for something that's beyond the horizon. To roam, and explore, is ingrained deeply within the human spirit and psyche for centuries before & for those to come. So, travel, travel, travel. Just take that first step to book your tickets and then go ahead & pack your bags!

Ikigai & Other Japanese Concepts

"Only staying active will make you want to live a hundred years"
— Japanese proverb

There's a word the Japanese use to describe why they get up in the morning with a spring in their step, even at 90 years old. That word is *Ikigai*—roughly translating to "a reason for being". In the modern age, we hear a lot about passion and purpose, but Ikigai goes deeper. Imagine a Venn diagram: In one circle, you have what you love; in another, what you're good at; in a third, what the world needs; and in the fourth, what you can be paid for. Your Ikigai sits at the center, waiting to be discovered. It's not always obvious, and it might take some digging, but once you find it, everything else begins to make sense. You start to see that your work isn't just about earning money, but rather, it's about contributing something meaningful to the world. And that's where true satisfaction lies.

Although the term Ikigai has been thrown around in popular culture these days, Hector Garcia and Francesc Miralles break this down in their book, titled *Ikigai* and it's nothing short of life-changing. Have you ever felt like you're just going through the motions? Work, eat, sleep, repeat. That's where Ikigai steps in, bringing clarity to the apparent banal fog. It's about finding something that makes every day feel worth living, not just surviving or living one day to the next meaninglessly.

The book highlights the people of Okinawa, Japan (a place known for its astonishing number of centenarians), who live by this principle. They don't retire like we do. In fact, they don't even have a word for retirement. They just keep doing what they love until their last breath, and that, is the secret ingredient.

In Okinawa, the sense of community is strong, and people take care of each other. It's part of their *Ikigai*. They garden, they sing, they walk daily, they eat plants, and they laugh—a lot. But the real magic comes from that deep-rooted sense of purpose. This doesn't mean you have to quit your 9-to-5 tomorrow.

Finding your Ikigai doesn't require a massive life overhaul. It's about finding joy in the small things, in the everyday. It's about recognising that your job might not be your passion, but it could be a vehicle to support what *is* your passion.

One of the core ideas from the book is to stay active, mentally and physically. Doing what you love is one part, but another is to never really "stop" & to keep moving. The older people in Okinawa don't just sit around waiting for their last days. They have rituals and hobbies, be it tending to their gardens, practising traditional crafts, or simply engaging with the community. It's all about *flow*— that state where you're so absorbed in what you're doing that time flies by (which I'll come to in a later chapter). Find that, and you're on your way to Ikigai.

In Japan, there's also a concept called *takumi*, referring to an artisan or master craftsman who has dedicated their life to perfecting their craft. The idea is that through consistent practice and commitment, one can reach a level of skill and artistry that transcends mere work and it becomes an expression of purpose. This resonates with *Ikigai* because *takumi* exemplifies the pursuit of excellence in a singular passion, merging what you love with what you're good at. Their meticulous attention to detail, patience, and dedication serve as a testament to the joy of mastery.

Finding your *Ikigai* doesn't mean rushing into various endeavours but honing in on those things you're willing to do repeatedly, improving day by day, just like a *takumi*.

The Okinawans, also practice *moai*, a social support network that encourages a sense of community and belonging, which plays a vital role in longevity and happiness. While *kaizen*, the principle of continuous improvement, also urges taking small, consistent steps toward personal growth.

This patient approach aligns beautifully with the Japanese philosophy of embracing imperfection, or *wabi-sabi*. In their book, Garcia and Miralles stress the importance of embracing imperfection. Life is messy, and that's okay. The Japanese word for this—*wabi-sabi*—which means finding beauty in the imperfect further explores how *Ikigai* can be found in the midst & perimeters of the imperfect.

Your Ikigai won't always be crystal clear, and you'll probably fail at a few things along the way. But each failure is just another step toward refining your purpose.

There's also *anti-fragility*—the idea that challenges and setbacks can make us stronger. Rather than avoiding adversity, those living by *Ikigai* embrace it, furthermore understanding that resilience is key to thriving. Combined with the joy of small, everyday pleasures, these principles offer a holistic way of life deeply rooted in balance and purpose.

This Is Sparta!

When King Philip II, the ruler of Macedon threatened to invade Sparta, the Spartans gave him a chilling response. Philip threatened with a note to the Spartans, saying, "If I enter Laconia, I will raze Sparta (to the ground)", to which the Spartans replied, "If". The Spartans were known to be fearsome warriors, but there's a wealth of things we can learn from the Spartans of old.

The Spartans weren't just warriors—they were the pinnacle of self-improvement. Feared by their enemies for their unmatched discipline, resilience, and mastery of warfare, Spartan society was built on one central ethos: excellence in every endeavour. But becoming a Spartan warrior wasn't just about learning to wield a sword & fight in combat. It was about becoming the best version of yourself, physically, mentally, and philosophically.

The path to Spartan mastery started early at the *agoge*. The *agoge* wasn't your typical education system, like we see today. Boys left their homes at an early age of around seven or eight to endure intense training in endurance, survival, combat, and group dynamics. This brutal schooling wasn't just to toughen them up, but to instill a lifelong commitment to self-discipline. From physical trials to critical thinking, everything was geared toward creating an elite warrior, but also a holistic individual capable of contributing to the state's greatness. And there was an artistry in their training too—poetry, music, philosophy—were key to shaping a well-rounded mind. This wasn't brutality for brutality's sake, Spartans believed that true mastery in life meant mastering both the body and mind.

One of the most gruelling tests of the *agoge* was the *krypteia*, where young men were sent into the wilderness with nothing but a knife, tasked with surviving and stalking *helots* (the enslaved class). This was less about the kill and more about honing stealth, resourcefulness, and independence. It was almost their version of a "final exam" & was a test of surviving alone in the wild. No pressure.

But while martial training was at the forefront of a Spartan youth's development, it's crucial to understand that Spartans cultivated the art of living. In fact, it was the way they blended poetry, dance, and philosophy with warcraft that made them so formidable.

Brett and Kate McKay in their book *The Spartan Way* explore how Spartans viewed physical hardship as just one facet of human development. Their success lay in mastering life's complexities with the same intensity they brought to the battlefield. In a sense, their pursuit was not just for victory in battle but victory over themselves i.e. complete mastery over mind, body, and spirit.

The Spartans also cultivated & fostered community with the *syssitia*. The *syssitia* was the cornerstone of Spartan communal life, channelling unity and camaraderie among the warriors. It was more than a mere dining club—it was a place where Spartans gathered for shared meals, discussions, and bonded.

Every male Spartan was required to participate, and the meals were simple, reinforcing the values of discipline and equality. The Spartan *syssitia* symbolised the collective over the individual, helping foster a sense of brotherhood that translated directly onto the battlefield. Spartans believed that this strong community connection was key to their military dominance.

In the *syssitia*, men ate, discussed strategy, and bonded over their common goals & conversation. This environment kept them grounded and reinforced the importance of shared responsibility and loyalty to the state. The communal nature of the *syssitia* also taught young Spartans to prioritise the needs of their comrades over their own, contributing to the deep sense of unity that was essential in the Spartan phalanx formation in battle. Each soldier relied on the man next to him, and this trust was nurtured around the dinner table.

The *syssitia* is a concept we can still apply today but of course, not exactly. Building community, whether at work, in social circles, or even in families, often revolves around the simple act of sharing a meal. The idea that strong communities are built on shared experiences is timeless, and the Spartans understood this.

There's little documented about the Spartans that survives today. But in the 21st century, we can look at the Spartan way as an exemplary way of self- development. Their relentless pursuit of perfection is not something many would sign up for, but there's a lesson in it that mastery isn't one-dimensional.

The same ethos can be applied to modern life. So whether you're trying to build a business, chase a personal goal, or just become a better version of yourself, mastery over yourself is the most crucial part. True greatness lies in pushing past your limitations in all aspects—intellectual, emotional, and physical. And while we may not be facing down enemies with a spear or sword, the lessons of Spartan mastery remind us that self-discipline, resilience, and continuous improvement are timeless paths to individual mastery. Furthermore, also urging that family & community are pillars of creating a wholesome life.

As Hunter S. Thompson's quote reads: "Walk tall, kick ass, learn to speak Arabic, love music and never forget you come from a long line of truth seekers, lovers and warriors."

The 2x Value Principle —Create Value in Your Work & Value Your Work

When you buy something, whatever the product or service is, the key thing any buyer looks for is value for the money they're spending. Even when buying stocks in the stock market as an investment or a home as an investment or for your family, value for the buck is the most critical aspect of the purchase.

Similarly, your life's work should be of value not just to you but to others as well. After a certain point of time, you'll eventually stop working just for making money & for the sake of making money, although most people usually always start off that way. But as you get older, you'll want your work to be of value, i.e. to actually align with your innate & inborn passions, interests & life goals. How you spend your time is totally up to you, but you've got to make sure it's worthwhile & valuable.

The 2x Value principle suggests two critical things — **creating value** with your work and **valuing the work** you do yourself. In a nutshell, you're creating value for others and creating satisfaction and fulfilment for yourself.

However, finding the perfect area to create value can be a slightly difficult task; it only comes with introspection and finding out what your innate & inborn passions and interests are and how skilled you are at them.

Ask yourself these introspective questions and then move to the checklist:

The Questions

i) What do I really want to do?

ii) What would I do if I had all the money & resources available?

iii)   What value does it give others?

iv)   What value does it give me?

The Checklist

i)   Do I feel what I'm doing is valuable to me?

ii)   Will I value the time I spend doing it?

iii)   Will it impact me and my family positively or negatively?

iv)   Will I value the process of working on it?

v)   Will I be willing to commit to it for 5-10 years at least?

vi)   Will I feel satisfied with what I did when I'm in the last years of my life or will I regret it?

Note down ten or more options for the first two questions. Once you've noted them all down, use the checklist as a box to check, be descriptive if you need to, but find the top three most valuable things using this system and ditch the rest.

Furthermore, don't be afraid to find areas of work that overlap. They can be broad, they can have congruences, they can be derived from experiences, what you've studied & your inclinations & so on.

For me, I narrowed it all down to four things — writing, music, film and football. I've hitched a career writing about football, music and film & working as a musician, producer, DJ and film composer. I found areas where they overlap and I've used my engineering background to explore how tech fits in these fields of work as well by venturing into music technology.

So yes, find your top three most valuable pursuits using the 2x value principle & you'll be on your way to your *Ikigai* & subsequently fulfilment.

Think of a Problem, Engineer A Solution

When it comes to a "why?" from the perspective of life, you need to find your own proper "why?" & why it is you do the things you want to do. However, from a business, career or entrepreneurial standpoint you need to solve some kind of problem if you are to create a successful startup or career. Solving a burgeoning problem that merges with your expertise & interest is the best way to build a business or career ground-up & impart your own identity to it.

This can be applied to doing particular jobs after finding out core problems as well. The crux is if you personally feel there's some kind of a gap or problem that you can solve better than others, using your knowledge & skills go ahead and do it.

For example, if you feel that movie reviews online aren't as in-depth & comprehensive as you think they should be, you can become a film critic or start a YouTube channel where you can solve that problem. If you feel that sports reports aren't as engaging & intensive i.e. covering tactics, in-game plays, strategies & coaching you can solve that problem by offering your expertise to a sports website or create a website or blog that does the same yourself. If you feel that companies are not recycling waste sustainably & efficiently in your area you could start an organisation that helps do that or if you feel the clothes sold by stores online aren't made with enough quality & aren't affordable you could start a clothing brand that caters to quality while being affordable. These are just some basic examples.

So, it helps to first identify, & think of a problem that needs solving. For example, in the broader sense, EVs were launched because we couldn't endlessly burn fossil fuels without leaving a carbon footprint. Renewables solved the same problem. In architecture, shorter 4-5 storied buildings grouped together offer better standards of living & help use solar & other utilities & facets better & more equitably as compared to giant skyscrapers.

Uber helped organise how to get a cab in the 21st century. UPI & wallets helped people transact cashlessly.

It helps to think about a problem that needs solving. And in turn, align it with your expertise, experience & inclinations. Innovation always stems from solving a problem in a unique way.

You don't have to be an engineer to engineer a solution to a problem. Anyone can play the role of a creative engineer or offer their expertise to solve a particular problem. But it's paramount to develop a way & system to find a problem & then, in turn, solve it.

Some steps you can follow are:

i) Understand what the core problem you're solving is & your personal experience with that problem

ii) Find out what's the best way to solve it using technology or otherwise

iii) Figure out what's the innovation behind it

iv) Assess its feasibility regionally, nationally or globally

v) See how it aligns with your knowledge & expertise

vi) Implement it

Education Doesn't Matter, Skills Do

"No Skill, No Kill" — *Unknown*

My grandfather was a principal of a school in Chennai, Tamil Nadu, India. He stressed and stressed and heavily advocated education in his lifetime.

He was a brilliant mathematician but was raised in a small village in Tamil Nadu during his youth, without access to great education. However, he eventually left home and moved to Chennai after marrying my grandmother and began working tediously towards raising his children, including my mother, and supporting his family after becoming a teacher and then later a principal.

He ensured that my mother and her other four siblings were well-educated. He used to encourage me to play chess as a child, but sadly passed away just before I finally finished my schooling and my mother often tells me stories of how brilliant & gifted and hardworking he was.

I come from an upper-middle-class family in Mumbai and was given access to a great education in my youth, which I'm forever grateful for. But what if you're born into poverty, your family can't afford to send you to school, or you've not had access to a proper education? This is largely apparent in a lot of remote villages in India and in a lot of third-world countries around the world (although that's slow changing).

However, you don't need a stellar education or degrees to live life to the fullest or make an income. Education really doesn't matter, but the skills you develop matter the most.

In developing a skill or several skills, you can then exchange your skills for money and that will ensure that you never die hungry. By mastering and developing skills, you can trade your expertise in that particular skill for money, food, housing and whatever your basic needs are.

Whatever the skill maybe, whether it's cooking, writing, learning to code & becoming an expert programmer, playing musical instruments, becoming a highly skilled athlete or sportsman, becoming an expert salesman or communicator, or coach or photographer, and the skill list goes on...

So whatever industry you wish to work in, just develop the relevant skills so that you can work in that particular industry and become **so highly skilled**, that **the industry simply cannot ignore you** because of your skill level.

Poverty is impermanent in this modern day and age when cell phones are a gateway to learning, and even the poorest households and kids can leverage technology like smart phones to become exceptionally skilled and develop skills that will, in turn, lead to monetary gain for their basic needs while serving as a way of uplifting themselves.

In this day and age, all you need is a cell phone to learn, and a lot of initiatives from companies, NGOs(non-profits) and the Indian government are enabling kids to learn and get an education via their cell phones; for example, a company called *Rocket Learning* where my younger sister is currently working.

On the other side of the spectrum, you have the kids who have the best education there is to offer in the world today. The likes of Harvard, Yale, Stanford, Oxford, LSE, abroad & IIT & ISB in India etc. Sure, they get high-paying jobs, and that stamp of graduating from those colleges but if they're not skilled enough they'll eventually fall behind.

That's privilege for you. But it's commonplace for them to get a cushy consulting job, or become comfy investment bankers and so on, but at the end of the day and sooner or later, their skills will come into question and despite having that "chappa" or "stamp" as we say in Mumbai slang, of having graduated from a top university they're not going to see exceptional growth or rise through the ranks of their jobs without at least one or more highly coveted skills. Whether that's leadership, networking, problem-solving, innovating or other slightly managerial-oriented skill sets, skills eventually matter the most.

Make Your Own Waves

But then there are also the innovators and visionaries, who despite having a privileged education, and getting accepted into a top university, have the cojones to drop out of Harvard and create value and disrupt industries. But they wouldn't be able to do that without skills.

Mark Zuckerberg was an exceptional programmer who built Facebook on a computer in his college dorm. The current Indian prime minister Narendra Modi was a "chaiwala", or "tea seller" in India and rose through the ranks of the BJP party, of course with his fair share of questionable decisions, to become the current Prime Minister of India. He is the complete example of the Indian dream & but his oratory and negotiation skills are exemplary.

I also wrote a blog post about a TED Talk by a farmer in Thailand named Jon Jandai(which I'll cover in detail in other chapters) who said 'screw it' to life in the city after being sent to Bangkok to study and returned to his village and learnt to build earthen houses, cook & sell food, & sew and knit clothes, and used those skills to uplift himself and create the life he wanted, by a scenic ocean. He built four houses for himself, and created an eco-village, all by simply learning and using his skills.

So don't fall prey to that narrative of being from a lesser fortunate background and moan about it because others got dealt a better hand than you. These are the cards that are dealt, do what you can with it…

Yes, the system needs to change, but at the end of the day, the playing field eventually evens out as time progresses, whether you're from a rich or middle class or poor background, the onus is on you to develop skills and trade them in to uplift yourself or become more well off and comfortable.

"No skill, no kill".

Start Where You Are with What You Have

The entire notion of feeling sorry for yourself because you were born with lesser than others is just a bad excuse. Suggesting that the head start others have had in life determines their eventual achievements is a fallacy and an appalling myth of the 21st century. Sure, privilege counts initially, but building on from the earlier section, your beginnings really don't matter in the grander scheme of things. There's you and your experiences and skills and you've got a lot to offer the world, but your mindset is preventing you from achieving all the great things you could achieve.

I couldn't advocate this more but starting with where you are and what you have is the only way to get going. Mumbai & India has this slang word called "jugaad", which is essentially, "to find a way". Whether you're struggling in life or contemplating starting something new and exciting or have a brilliant idea but seemingly no means to accomplish it, is where *jugaad* comes into play.

There are those people that exemplify *jugaad* and that just get it done, irrespective of:

    a) Not having enough money

    b) Not having well to do beginnings

    c) Not having enough resources

    d) Not having a good enough education

    e) Not having a stable job or roof over their head

It really could go on, but there are just those people who find a way to get things done while the others crib and moan about all the reasons they can't do it, instead of focussing on the ways they can do it.

Some people will give you 10 problems for every solution you think of, the pessimists, the cautious ones, the conformists, people who are afraid to take a leap into the unknown in place of comfort, the people who shoot you and your dreams down by their limited and narrow mindset.

So, if you have something you want to accomplish, just "find a way". Do what you need to, but get it done.

There are a couple of ways to do this — either by yourself or in true entrepreneurial spirit, which is totally aligned with *jugaad*, find others to do it for you in a cleverly coaxed or disguised way.

You need to leverage your contacts and your experience to create and make your idea(s) come to life. True *jugaad* comes from the will to get things done despite the setbacks and difficulties. *Jugaad* embodies the street-smart way of getting things done & finding ways to progress beyond the conventional. It involves out-of-the-box thinking and in general, a way to find solutions and solve problems in a unique way. The essence of progress stems from tireless persistence and using *jugaad* to create positive outcomes & progress through each stage until your idea comes to life.

You could write a hundred business plans, you could have the best idea, you could do all the research, but if you don't get it done, it's going to be a failure.

Research and business plans are pretty overrated, they're buzz terms and expected normalities & formalities in entrepreneurial and business circles. Sure, it's good to know your target market and how you plan to make income, and apart from a basic understanding of the idea, product or service and market, which you really don't need heavy documentation on, it all depends on taking things forward and making it happen. There's no chance in hell that your business is going to go exactly as you drafted and planned it in your business plan. Not a chance; you have to adapt and innovate.

Unless you actually "do it" & "get started" and get the ball rolling, with whatever resources you have at your disposal, i.e. where you are and what you have, it's just going to be another piece of paper that didn't make it out of the drawing board.

Some of the most disruptive ideas have been met with surprisingly high resistance.

And most seed angels and VCs will only put in their funds if they see income, growth or popularity. VCs just want an entry and exit and to make a profit.

That's the case with most VCs and funds you'll find. The rarities are VCs and angels that actually believe in your vision and story and idea; 95% of them won't.

Most companies don't last the 40 year life cycle. Think of any company.

But for every 10 ideas that fail, there's one which could succeed. So, perseverance matters as well. Sure ideas can change the world, but ideas are also cheap, and getting it done matters most.

The key here is to get started with where you are & what you have i.e. your expertise, experience & resources, and find ways to get things done despite the problems, setbacks & difficulties that might arise.

Breaking down the barriers that could prevent your progress and most importantly bringing your idea to life despite those barriers matters the most. In most cases, building an MVP (minimum viable product) is the first step and things follow soon after it. So, it's just about getting off the drawing board and bringing something to life in its most crude form that's the first step.

As long as you can get it done, adapt and innovate and most importantly identify and solve a problem and create value, you're on the right track.

And as I've elucidated, just "get that sh*t done" and find a way with who you are, what your background is, where you are, and with what you have, in the true spirit of *jugaad.*

Although I've explained this in business terms, it could be for anything you wish to do. Whatever it might be: a job, a skill, a passion, a side business, a social project, a relationship, a dream, you need to just start where you are with what you have; the key being to *take the risk*, to *start & finish* and just *get it done.*

Perseverance & Grit Will See You Through

"Fall down seven times, stand up eight." - Chinese Proverb

Life is full of setbacks, obstacles and tough times. As the age-old saying goes, "tough times don't last, tough people do," — but in essence it's all about perseverance. In the peaks and crevices of life, what matters most is how you react and respond to setbacks and failures. Failures teach you more about yourself and your mindset than your success. The most important traits that most psychologists identify with people who overcome their troubles and become outliers in their industries or pursuits are perseverance and grit.

In Japanese culture and philosophy, the saying is *"Nana korobi ya oki"* (literally meaning: seven falls, eight getting up). This is an integral part of Japanese culture which is represented in their business, sports, education, martial arts and one of the touchstones of Zen practice.

Japanese people also call this *"ganbaru",* based on an ancient Samurai principle which means to "persist" or "persevere" and dedicate oneself to a task and accomplish it with tenacity & make constant and persistent effort to complete the task no matter how difficult and no matter how many obstacles and hurdles you find on the way.

As I've explained in one of the earlier chapters using the football analogy, how you react and respond to being knocked down by life determines how your life will be. Giving up is easy, but working at it, constantly making progress and persevering is a critical aspect of living life.

Most people are familiar with the movie *Rocky* created by Sylvester Stallone, who himself has had his fair share of troubles & tough times.

Stallone had no money for food and had to sell his dog for $50 just so he could buy food. After he wrote the script for the first *Rocky* film and successfully got it approved by a studio, he bought his dog back & the rest is history.

In the 2006 edition of the film's series there's an interesting speech he makes, in which he says:

"The world ain't all sunshine and rainbows. It is a very mean and nasty place and it will beat you to your knees and keep you there permanently if you let it. You, me, or nobody is gonna hit as hard as life. But it ain't how hard you hit; it's about how hard you can get hit, and keep moving forward. How much you can take, and keep moving forward. That's how winning is done. Now, if you know what you're worth, then go out and get what you're worth. But you gotta be willing to take the hit, and not pointing fingers saying you ain't where you are because of him, or her, or anybody. Cowards do that and that ain't you. You're better than that!"

That's perhaps the most important thing in life; to take the hits and keep moving forward. Another inspirational story about grit and perseverance is in the life story of Glenn Cunningham - a middle-distance runner, widely regarded as the greatest American miler of all time.

Cunnigham was born in Atlanta, Kansas on August 4th, 1909. When he was eight years old, he got severely burnt in an accidental gasoline fire in his school which took the life of his brother Floyd. Cunningham had severe burns all over his lower body and doctors in the hospital gave him little chance of surviving, but he did.

The story doesn't end there, because of the severity of his injuries and burns, doctors told Cunningham's parents that he would never walk again.

After he was released from the hospital, he went back to live with his mother & father. His doting parents would massage his legs every day, and for a considerable amount of time, he could feel no sensation in his legs. His mother used to wheel him out to their backyard in a wheelchair to take him outside for fresh air.

Then one day, Cunningham did something extraordinary; he decided to get out of his wheelchair and he threw himself on the grass and pulled his body across the lawn dragging his legs to the fence. Periodically, he did the same thing every day and began to drag himself along the fence in his backyard. With daily massage therapy and dragging himself along the fence, with the sheer grit and will to walk again, Cunningham's legs began to function and the strength in his legs began to be restored and eventually, he began to walk again and then run.

Recounting his struggle, Cunnigham later said, "It hurt like thunder to walk, but it didn't hurt at all when I ran. So for five or six years, about all I did was run."

Eventually, Cunningham became a middle-distance runner and was selected for his university track and field team. For three years between 1932-34 he won the big six indoor running titles and represented the USA at two Olympics winning a silver medal at the 1936 Olympics in Berlin. Then in 1938, he broke the world record for an indoor mile run clocking 4:04.4.

Although his world record would get beaten, he was aptly dubbed as "The Kansas Ironman". His story is perhaps the greatest example of perseverance & grit. He was given no chance of walking, but in the end, his sheer will and determination he became one of the greatest runners in American history.

This incredible story reflects on just how important grit and perseverance are & with the will to conquer and succeed, grit and perseverance will see you through. Whatever your situation may be, whatever the struggle, the obstacles, the failure, it's up to you to never give up and relentlessly keep moving forward and persevere.

Life is transient, there are the ebbs and flows which are bitter and pleasurable. But whatever happens in your life, you've got to take the bull by its horns and fight and overcome whatever problems you face, whether that's from tragedy, financial loss, business failure, failed relationships, career hurdles, mistakes, wrongdoing or whatever it might be.

Perseverance and grit will see you through…

Response To Failure Is Paramount - An Exploration By Robert H. Schuller

As I've partly touched upon in the earlier chapter on perseverance and *'ganbaru'*, perseverance is a cornerstone of the broader idea of response to failure. This chapter is based on Robert H. Schuller's book *Success Is Never Ending, Failure Is Never Final* wherein, as the title suggests, 'failure is never final'. You've probably heard this a lot, but to truly grasp it is essential because life is full of mixed experiences & there will be difficult times, but how you respond & react to setbacks, failures, and bad times, determines who you are. You need to truly grasp that failure isn't permanent & that there's always time for a turnaround.

In *Success Is Never Ending, Failure Is Never Final*, Robert H. Schuller stresses on the importance of resilience and how our response to failure shapes the trajectory of our lives. He shares numerous stories of individuals who faced adversity but chose to persevere like Thomas Edison and Walt Disney, underlining that setbacks are not the end of the road but opportunities for growth. Schuller advocates for seeing failure as a stepping stone to future success, urging that your attitude and ability to bounce back are key. The right mindset can transform failure into a valuable learning experience, leading to eventual triumph.

The essence of Robert H. Schuller's book, lies in one central truth: how we respond to failure is far more important than the failure itself. Schuller explores the delicate relationship between success and failure, presenting the argument that failure, though often seen as final and debilitating, is a necessary part of success.

In the key stories from the book, Schuller recounts how successful people, from athletes to business leaders, often had moments of great despair before they found triumph. Schuller highlights figures like Thomas Edison, who failed thousands of times before inventing the lightbulb, and

Walt Disney on bringing his vision of *Disney* to life, to demonstrate that persistence is the key to lasting success.

The core principle that Schuller urges us to grasp is that *our reaction to failure is paramount*. Those who view failure as a definitive end often find themselves stuck, unable to move forward, whereas those who view it as a temporary setback maintain their momentum. In this way, the book is less about external achievements and more about the internal resilience required to overcome life's inevitable obstacles. More importantly, your internal dialogue in times of failure is paramount.

Schuller presents failure as an opportunity to reimagine goals, sharpen our focus, and refine our approach. He argues that the greatest achievements in life often come after profound failures, because in those moments, we learn the most about ourselves and what we are capable of.

In essence, *Success Is Never Ending, Failure Is Never Final* teaches us that success is not a straight line, but a winding path filled with detours and dead ends. The graph isn't linear but full of crests & troughs. The ultimate takeaway is that **the story isn't over until we decide it is.** The power of resilience, and more importantly, the faith to push through adversity, and the mindset to learn from our failures are what truly make the difference in the pursuit of success, whatever your definition of success may be.

Robert H. Schuller's *Success Is Never Ending, Failure Is Never Final* is structured around key ideas meant to inspire resilience and perseverance. The core concepts of the book are:

1. The Power of Possibility Thinking

In the opening chapters, Schuller promotes "Possibility Thinking," which is rooted in the belief that success is attainable for anyone willing to think beyond limitations. This mindset helps individuals unlock creative solutions, turning obstacles into opportunities. Schuller explores how adopting this attitude is essential for overcoming failures and achieving long-term success.

2. Failure as a Stepping Stone

A central theme in the book is that failure is an inevitable part of the journey toward success. Schuller urges that failures should be viewed as temporary setbacks rather than permanent defeats. Instead of being deterred by failure you've got to embrace it as a stepping stone on the path to greater achievement.

3. Goal Setting and Vision

Schuller explains the importance of clear goals and a strong vision. He argues that success requires both short-term and long-term goals. By having a clear vision, individuals are able to focus their energy and efforts in the right direction, ensuring they continue moving forward, even after encountering failures. Vision serves as a guiding path, providing motivation and clarity during difficult times.

4. Faith and Positive Action

The book places a heavy emphasis on the role of faith—both spiritual and personal. Schuller suggests that faith gives individuals the confidence to move forward, even in uncertain times. Alongside faith, positive action is crucial.

Schuller believes that success requires not only optimism but also the discipline to take consistent, purposeful action.

5. Turning Adversity into Advantage

Another key concept is transforming **adversity into advantage**. Schuller shares stories of people who faced hardship but used their setbacks to pivot toward greater success. The idea is that challenges often contain hidden opportunities, and it is through adversity that people can discover new strengths, skills, or paths they may not have otherwise explored.

6. The Importance of Perseverance

Schuller discusses how **perseverance is the most critical factor** in achieving lasting success. He explores the importance of not giving up, even when faced with repeated failures or difficulties. It encourages people to stay committed to their goals, reminding them that the darkest moments often precede the biggest breakthroughs.

7. **Success Is a Journey, Not a Destination**

One of the book's final concepts is the idea that success is not a final, static achievement but an ongoing process. Schuller argues that true success is found in the continual pursuit of one's goals, personal growth, and fulfilment. Rather than focusing solely on reaching a specific milestone, individuals should **embrace the journey itself** and the growth in all areas of life. Furthermore, we need to keep reinventing ourselves & our goals & definition of success, because as Schopenhauer's thought reveals in the earlier chapter, we should ensure that there's no end to our goal to live a more fulfilled life.

8. **Overcoming Fear**

In the later chapters, Schuller discusses the role of fear in preventing success. He suggests that **fear of failure is often what holds people back from achieving their true potential**. Overcoming this fear requires self-belief, positive thinking, and a willingness to take calculated risks because fear kills off more success & glory than failure ever can.

9. **Legacy and Long-term Success**

The book concludes by addressing the concept of legacy and how true success extends beyond personal achievements. Schuller encourages readers to think about how they can contribute to the greater good, building a legacy that positively impacts others long after they are gone. Success is not just about personal gain but about leaving a meaningful mark on the world (which I will elucidate in detail in another chapter towards the end of this book).

Sometimes, failure can be a way to tearing down an old approach and adapting and reinventing it into something new. At times, the only way forward is to tear down what isn't working in favour of something that does. In this sense, failure can serve as a way of reimagining our motives and targets & thinking outside the box to create something worthwhile. It urges a rethink and propels us in the direction we need to be heading in by discarding what isn't working.

To Schuller, the response to failure is not just about pushing forward aimlessly, but about reflecting, learning, and adapting. Those who can master this approach will find that, *our response to failure is paramount* & furthermore that, *failure is never final* unless we view it as the final nail in the coffin of our progress or goals or whatever we're aiming to achieve.

La Pausa: The Importance of Pause

Picture this. You're eating your daily lunch but instead of eating your food mindfully, your mind is constantly drifting to all kinds of work-related thoughts.

Drafting that proposal or presentation, contacting that investor, that client meeting or that pending task at work, that Google Meet call, that journey back home after office hours & worrying about the traffic, what time you need to leave, what time you need to reach home for dinner. By the time you know it, you've finished your lunch. You're full, but are you satisfied, fulfilled & happy?

All you had to do was the simple act of eating lunch mindfully & deliberately only focusing on your food, for a *pause*.

It's a commonplace example which we all can relate to. We have similar thoughts weighing on us that prevent us from being mindful & living in the moment and the essential *'pauses'* we need in life.

It's these *pauses* that are usually very important as we proceed to live our lives and as we age.

If we don't take time to pause every now and then, life is going to pass us by really fast. We live life at such a high octane speed in this modern era like Usain Bolt (the world's fastest man) pushing himself from the start to that extra bit to win his 100-meter dash.

Life is not a 100-meter sprint. And even Usain Bolt can't run several 100-meter races one after another.

We all need to pause every once in a while and just do — nothing.

Shortly after the COVID pandemic, as normalcy began to be restored to everyday life, I found myself in hyper-productive mode. 2022 was a hyper-productive year for me — I released a book, put out several EPs & LPs as a producer under my stage name 'Ghost Intent', worked on 20+ short film scores as a composer, enrolled in a programming course & launched a content startup after developing the website myself, apart from all the investor & client meetings, team recruitment, daily work on the platform and regularly practising the guitar & piano & posting covers on Instagram (although that's my fall back space which I like to turn to in my downtime).

But I was still constantly at it all, day after day, minute after minute, just work & all the planning, execution and worrisome aspects of running a startup, and even making music in my free time, was creatively & fully exhausting me.

It continued into February 2023. But by mid-Feb, I was completely exhausted & was suffering from considerable burnout. I was totally exhausted with everything going on in my life. That's when I decided that I just needed a break.

I put everything on hold & decided to travel to my favourite beach destination in India — Gokarna.

As soon as I reached and saw the sunrise over the hills on Om Beach, it stirred something inside me, and I was at complete peace & ever so relaxed. For the first few days, I barely even looked at my phone except to play music & take pictures & videos. I decided to put all my work & work related thoughts & worries aside & just focus on myself & let the ocean's unerring waves & its calm slowly seep into my mind & bring me peace.

I used this time to just sit by a view of the ocean at the wonderfully picturesque homestay I booked. I ate & drank mindfully by just focusing on the food & the view (there's something about the calmness of the waves & the light blue water & the way the sunlight shines on the sea's surface and makes the droplets dance like stars on the ocean surface as the sun leaves a trail of burning light through the centre of the sea). The sea is peace & the shoreline is home, for me.

Modern life goes by rather fast, and we miss all the good things if we don't take time to pause every now and then. But how can we create this space in our lives to give ourselves rest?

First, we must understand a few common facets of modern life.

Extractivism

We've become extractors, relentlessly drawing out every drop of value from moments, much like we've done with the planet's resources. Society's model mirrors our treatment of nature—coal, forests, animals—exploited without pause, driven by short-term gains. And now, we apply the same mindset to time, viewing it as something to be squeezed, and maximised.

But to shift this destructive paradigm, we must first reshape our internal world. This begins by reimagining time itself, not as something to extract from, but as a living rhythm to harmonise with. And at the essence of this is learning to cultivate *pause*.

Efficiency and Productivity

In the pursuit of productivity, we've forgotten we're not machines. We treat time as a non-stop resource to manage and optimise, resulting in a near-constant anxiety to do more, faster. But perhaps we're asking the wrong question. Nature, with its cycles—seasons, moon phases, circadian rhythms— reminds us that life thrives on a balance between activity and rest. Embracing these natural rhythms invites a gentler approach, where efficiency doesn't mean cramming more into each moment, but knowing when to *pause* and recharge.

We're more productive after taking short breaks. Our bodies are wired to perform more productively after taking these breaks. No musician can play an entire concert of songs without taking breaks.

Breaks, pauses, reflection, relaxing, reading, & at times just doing absolutely nothing, are much-needed & necessary ways to spend our time.

We need to divide our work into two segments:

Productive Work

In the realm of creation & execution, productive work is the hands-on, action-driven process of turning ideas into reality. It's the administrative, communicative, and collaborative effort which serves as the meeting ground where thoughts meet execution. However, when we fixate solely on productivity, we risk burnout, drowning in the noise & what the activity of constant doing entails.

Reflective Work

Reflective work, on the other hand, is the quiet pause between those actions. It's the space where ideas are born. These are the "shower thought" moments, the creative sparks that arrive when we stop trying to produce & when we just 'are'. If you're a creative person, you've probably found ideas popping up in your head out of nowhere when you're just about to go to bed, or at random moments when you're doing nothing. We've all been there (a good practice is to note them down on your phone or somewhere so that the idea isn't lost). But when we detach from the grind, our minds are free to wander and synthesise thoughts without pressure.

Finding the Rhythm Between Productive & Reflective Work

So, how do we strike the balance between relentless productivity and quiet reflection? I'd like to think of the approach like scoring the music of a film—the big, dramatic moments wouldn't feel as powerful without the soft, ambient build-ups in between and of course the silences & pauses.

There are moments when the score swells, pushing the story forward & accentuating the scene, and other times when it pulls back, allowing the scene to breathe. If you're always pushing the music too loud or too frequently, you drown out the subtleties & it becomes too heavy to process for audiences. And if you hold back too much, you lose momentum. It's about knowing when to add music and when to let the silence speak. That's the best way to balance our lifestyle — the moments to swell, the moments of consistent rhythm and the moments to let silence & pauses speak.

It's absolutely paramount to go slow & take things easy & more essentially de-clutter our minds & relax our bodies so that we can perform better when we need to. Mindfulness & meditation & other breathing techniques or just spending time with nature with a pristine view & some healthy food & juice can do wonders.

Here are some activities we can do to cultivate *pause*:

Engage in aimless activities: Carve out moments for the seemingly "pointless", whether it's a quiet walk, staring out the window, or fiddling with a small object. These activities, without a defined end goal, can reset & nourish the mind & body by celebrating the beauty of the process, doing nothing.

Leave space for organic creativity: Not every action must answer the demands of life. Leave gaps in your agenda for the work that bubbles up naturally from within, i.e. work that answers not to urgency, but to authenticity & introspection & reflection.

Breathe to reset: Start your day with deliberate breathing & conscious breathing exercises. These quiet moments of connection with your body serve as resets before and between the rush of meetings & work you have to do.

Heed the signs of overwhelm: Stress is often a signal from within, asking us to *pause*. When the world feels heavy, step back and give yourself the space to reflect, and to simply be.

Walking in Nature: Sometimes, the simplest things like stepping outside can remind us that we are a part of something larger and grander; an extension of nature itself. Staring at leaves, the endless sky, and listening to birds singing all serve as quiet reminders of the rhythms beyond our rush.

Journaling: Putting pen to paper is like having a quiet conversation with yourself. In the process, you can write whatever you'd like to jot down & capture the fleeting, the forgotten, and the overlooked thoughts we might miss if we're only working.

Art Appreciation: Whether it's standing before a painting or losing yourself in a film, or music, moments spent with art help slow the mundane & breathe life into our moments. They invite us to feel and think beyond the immediacy of what's going on & as I've explored in detail in the earlier chapter, it can breathe life into the mundane.

Travel to reconnect: Just like I did with my impromptu trip to Gokarna, journeying beyond our routines, whether to a distant place, a shoreline or mountain or hillside or even a nearby park, offers an effective reset.

Travelling to reconnect & *pause* invites new perspectives, quiets the internal noise, and is a reminder of the expansive beauty that lies beyond our daily grind & need for productivity.

So essentially, most of us are living at breakneck speed, and that can hamper our well-being. We can't expect to work like clockwork and the importance of taking a step back, relaxing & winding down when it's required is necessary as we aim to be more productive with our ideas, goals and work.

It's all about balance. And taking a break is as requisite as eating every day. So remember to do it mindfully & with *pause*.

No Risk, No Reward Lessons Learned From 'The Big Short'

Director & screenwriter Adam McKay made history, making a film about history, in what was an account of the biggest bet in history. *The Big Short* is easily one of the greatest movies ever made in the corporate/business film genre, and might I add one of the coolest.

For those of you who don't know what the film *The Big Short* is about, it's a 2015 film based on Michael Lewis' book, chronicling the lead-up to the 2008 global financial crisis. The plot follows several unconventional & bordering on oddball finance experts, like Michael Burry (Christian Bale) and Mark Baum (Steve Carell), & several others who predict the housing bubble collapse. These outsiders bet against the housing market by investing in credit default swaps, a financial instrument designed to profit from the inevitable crash. Despite widespread scepticism, their bold moves pay off, but at the cost of devastating economic fallout for millions & the film highlights systemic greed and ignorance in the global financial sector & system.

While I could go on about the film here are some learnings from it. They border on philosophical, albeit slightly generic, but could just hit home for you.

#1 It's Paramount To Ask — Always Ask
After Christian Bale's character, Michael Burry finds out that there's an asset bubble that would lead to the meltdown and crash of the US real estate market, he acts on his discovery by using a bit of inspired brilliance. Burry travels to New York and meets the boards of several financial institutions on Wall Street and engineers his own financial product called the **credit default swap**, an instrument which is a kind of contract linked

to the CDO or collateralised debt obligation (CDOs) so that he can short the housing market.

The key takeaway here is that Burry went out of the conventions & norms of how systems work (in this case the financial system) and decided to ask if he could get what he wanted. If you don't ask, you don't get it; it's that simple.

Burry created his own financial instrument to take his short position; something few people throughout history can boast.

So, if it's that raise, promotion, new job, bargaining, or it's that travel plan with someone, or asking that girl out on a date…. you've got to ask… or if it's that business idea, investor pitch or making that song, album, film and it requires something you need from others, you've got to ask people for it if you need to get it done. What's the worst that could happen? Rejection, that's it.

Message #1 — You've got to ask.

#2 Do Your Research

Being informed, aware & improving your knowledge every day is perhaps paramount. Burry does his in-depth research to uncover the impending real estate market meltdown, while Mark Baum played by Steve Carrell, another hedge-fund honcho who is more pragmatic, does some proper & extensive research by conducting field visits to various states across America. There he finds that loans have been issued despite being high-risk and with high chances of default.

Baum validates the truth about their then-speculated impending market crash by doing his own investigation. This comes shortly after Deutsche Bank executive Jared Vennett played by Ryan Gosling informs him about it.

(The character Mark Baum was based on the hedge fund manager Steve Eisman while Jared Vennett was based on Greg Lippmann, an ex-Deutsche Bank bond salesman)

Message #2 — Do your research & study, study, study

#3 Take Risks

You're born either rich, poor or middle-class. It's just the hand that's dealt. But what you do with the cards you're dealt determines your financial future & who you are.

Speaking about the cards that are dealt: you've got to take risks and gamble in different areas of your life i.e. take chances. You get nowhere by playing it safe. You've got to take risks, calculated risks to a certain degree depending on your risk appetite, but you've got to get out of your comfort zone and make some bold & risky moves, whatever they may be.

In the film, all the major characters bet millions via their short positions using Burry's engineered credit default swaps after they learn about them, and understand the high chances of the market crash to come. It was a huge gamble but backed by reasoning & proof. There were still chances of significant losses & it backfiring spectacularly; but that's gambling for you (I'm of course not talking about gambling games like rummy and poker but taking risks in other aspects of life, whatever they may be).

A lot of India's youth & people working hand-to-mouth jobs spend a lot of their time gaming on their phones or scrolling through or posting on social media. It really doesn't get them anywhere, and they often find it hard to break out of their predicament.

But it has more to do with them not taking risks, being careless with their time, lacking drive & ambition, settling for less, complaining about their problems and not doing anything about it. A lot of them work hard but they just waste their time otherwise; they stay where they are because they don't take risks.

So be mindful of your time, it's your greatest resource, and take some risks. Step by step.

Message #3 — you've got to take risks.

#4 Every Crisis Is An Opportunity

There are always lessons, learning and opportunities in crisis; whatever they may be. In an earlier chapter, I wrote about how spending time in concentration camps and exploring art turned revelatory for several holocaust survivors, even though it was their darkest hour.

That's an extreme example but whatever crisis happens, happened or could happen in our lives leads to life lessons but there's always a glimmer of opportunity if you look deep enough.

In terms of this story i.e. the extension to this story, which happened in real life — the second wave of people who began to short markets all over the world after the crisis went global in 2008, realised this. They did so by understanding the huge opportunity in the midst of this worldwide crisis.

While a lot of people created a furore in the news about the tanking of global markets, the irresponsibility of banks, and its repercussions while also scorning at the global layoffs worldwide, there was the opportunity to make some money, which the second wave of people realised this.

They used the opportunity presented by this market crash instead of joining the bandwagon of managers & civilians who were all just complaining. So being an opportunist and looking for the hidden opportunity amid crisis is a hallmark of intelligence.

Message #4 - find opportunity in crisis & learn lessons from it.

#5 Celebrate The Win But Don't Lose Your Head, Humility & Integrity

An important message McKay depicts in the film is when Charlie Geller (John Magaro) and Jamie Shipley (Finn Wittrock) two 20-somethings who run a small investment firm begin to celebrate their winnings vociferously & in an unwitting and over the top fashion. The pair discover a message written on tissue by Vennett (Ryan Gosling) that alerts them about credit default swaps and the opportunity to short the market. They then seek the advice and perspective of a retired banker named Ben Rickert (Brad Pitt) who lives in Singapore.

But despite the trio capitalising on the crash, Rickert lambasts the two youngsters for celebrating their success fervently. Rickert reminds the duo that Americans at the lowest strata of society in the USA would bear the brunt of the crisis and the money the trio managed to make, came at their cost.

While business is business, and you've got to be clever, being aware & humble about the truth is a sign of maturity & so is not letting your success get to your head.

This theme is echoed again as Baum books his profit eventually towards the end of the film, & is pictured being rather sad & mournful despite earning millions from his bet.

So, celebrate, celebrate your wins by all means, whatever they might be, but be humble and mindful of the reality and the different sides to the story & stay humble yourself.

Message #5 — celebrate the wins but stay humble & aware

#6 Always Go In The Opposite Direction To The Crowd

You've got to be different in life. You're made different, so why act like you're the same as everyone else? You've got something to offer the world in your own unique capacity, that only you can. So do that!

You've got to go in the opposite direction to the crowd. You can't be in the top 5% of the world: whether that's in terms of net worth, professionally in your particular industry, or in expertise of the field of your work by doing what everyone else is doing and thinking like everyone else.

This is brought to light majorly in the film. All the characters are all oddballs, outsiders and misfits; at least that's how the movie portrays them. But they go left when everyone goes right.

The way is inward, the way is within and the way is the different path we take alone. So remember to take the journey that not everyone takes and the path that not everybody takes as well.

Message #6 - go against the crowd

Practice, Practice, Practice - How Habits Make You & Why Practice Is Essential

"Amateurs call it genius; masters call it practice" — *Unknown*

Ask any musician or sports athlete at the top of their game, and they'll tell you how important & essential practice is. This chapter isn't what it seems if you read it until the end; to remodel the old Shakespeare quote— 'to practice or not to practice, that is the question'.

But first, I'll start with why practice is important & why we should aim for excellence through practice. There's a hidden power in repetition, in giving system to the mundane rhythm of life by practice & our daily habits shape who we become. This isn't a glamorous process, but it's vital. Malcolm Gladwell in his book *Outliers* highlights how greatness is built on the back of consistent practice, citing The Beatles' Hamburg years.

Long before they became global icons of music, The Beatles honed their craft by playing eight-hour sets, night after night in pubs in Hamburg. The relentless routine of playing in the Hamburg night scene gave them thousands of hours to perfect their sound, turning their raw talent into a perfectly tight band with a near perfect sound. Although I'm not the biggest Beatles fan, it's hard not to acknowledge them as one of the greatest bands of all time. But their so-called "overnight success" was anything but overnight—it was practice, practice, practice.

Gladwell's famous *10,000-hour rule* underscores this further i.e. to become truly world-class at anything, one must invest at least 10,000 hours of practice, it's become commonplace knowledge now. This isn't just about musical genius; it applies to businessmen, chess masters, dentists & doctors, gamers, athletes, and even Nobel Prize-winning scientists. Mastery, in this view, isn't some divine blessing. It's persistence, endurance, and a willingness to grind through the drudgery of improvement.

James Clear, in his book *Atomic Habits*, takes this philosophy a step further by breaking down how small, consistent actions compound over time to yield extraordinary results. Clear illustrates this with the concept of "the aggregation of marginal gains", where improving by just 1% every day leads to monumental changes over the course of a year.

Habits, Clear argues, are the building blocks of our lives. It's not just about the monumental goals but the tiny, daily actions that make up who we are. What you do every day matters more than what you do once in a while.

According to Clear, the key lies in systems, not goals. Goals give us direction, but systems, i.e. the habits we nurture, are what keep us moving. It's not enough to aim for the stars if you're not building a rocket one piece at a time. As Clear explains, "You do not rise to the level of your goals. You fall to the level of your systems."

A habit, then, is a ritual of improvement. Clear's habit loop describes this in detail. The habit loop comprises four elements: cue, craving, response, and reward. Every habit follows this cycle, whether it's brushing your teeth, practicing an instrument or writing a book.

The key to making habits stick is understanding and mastering this loop, which helps make even the smallest effort sustainable. When we embrace small improvements—whether it's reading a single page of a book daily or taking five minutes to meditate—we set ourselves up for success in the long run. In many cases, I've found in my experience, is that half the battle is to just *'start'*. As long as you make a conscious decision to start, you're halfway there already.

But it's also important that you *'finish'*.

Most times, we set up grandiose goals and targets and never hit them, but it's more often than not 'perfectionism' that's the scourge of progress & the act of finishing or hitting a target. In his book *Finish: Give Yourself the Gift of Done* Jon Acuff explores how trying to be perfect & setting elaborate goals can affect the slow and steady process ingrained in achieving goals and targets & eventual mastery.

Some of his strategies are profound but they underpin that "perfectionism kills progress". He also suggests breaking down goals and setting more achievable smaller goals and targets. One particular strategy is to cut the goal in half. So if you want to run 10 kilometres a day. Start by running 5 first. Or if you aim to write a book by writing 1000 words a day, start first by writing 500 a day.

But coming back, combining Gladwell's *10,000-hour rule* with Clear's idea of marginal gains, one thing becomes pretty clear i.e. that mastery isn't by chance, and transformation isn't instantaneous. Even late basketball legend Kobe Bryant revealed that the hours he put into practice oftentimes ditching his friends & parties in his younger years to practice on the court instead made his actual in-game performance better. Bryant attributed his relentless drive to practice to his success i.e. what seemed like effortless & clinch performances especially in big games throughout his time playing for the LA Lakers.

The core of it lies in the consistent, almost invisible acts of showing up, of trying again, and of trusting that each step forward, even the small ones, builds something far greater than the sum of its parts.

But should we take the effort to toil at practice, or is it even necessary at all?

The question of whether you should engage in practice, or refrain from it, can be viewed through several philosophical lenses. Aristotle, for starters, believed that *arete* (excellence) is achieved through habitual practice. According to him, we become virtuous through repeated action—virtue is not innate but cultivated over time. "We are what we repeatedly do. Excellence, then, is not an act but a habit," he famously said.

This highlights a key argument in favour of practice in that it shapes character, making you more capable and virtuous. Just like the Spartans (as explored in the earlier chapter) believed, self-mastery was the aim.

But on the other hand, existentialists like Jean-Paul Sartre challenged this automatic embrace of practice. Sartre was a proponent of *radical freedom*, suggesting that human beings are condemned to be free, meaning that we are not bound by patterns or habits unless we choose to be. To mindlessly follow repetitive action may, in this light, be a form of bad practice, where we deny our own freedom by becoming automatons of routine.

However, even for Sartre, choice is central. Engaging in practice becomes valuable when it's a conscious act of commitment. If you choose to practice a skill, the repetitive nature doesn't negate freedom but affirms it, as long as you're aware of the responsibility of that choice. Furthermore, in life we should aim to be the best versions of ourselves. But even if you don't want to do that or put in the hours of time & dedication to be the best version of yourself, inevitably, it's practice that shapes us.

Martin Heidegger's concept of *being-in-the-world* comes to the fore here. Heidegger argued that we are always already engaged in the world through action. As we practice, whether it's playing an instrument, solving problems, or improving at our job, those repeated actions become ingrained in our identity & attributes & selves. As time passes, the habits we engage in create neural pathways in the brain, much like grooves on a record.

This is the *process of becoming*: who you are today is a direct consequence of the things you've consistently done before that. In this sense, practice isn't just what we do; it becomes who we are.

Philosopher William James also lent a voice to this discussion, with his notion of *habit* as the flywheel of society. James believed that while free will allows us to make decisions, it is habit that drives human behaviour most of the time.

This gives a psychological foundation to the argument that practice is the engine behind much of human growth and improvement. Imagine if the early pioneers who built computers we have today, simply chose not to engage in mastering the technology.

We wouldn't have any of the technology we have today if they chose not to practice & master developing the technology. So practice, then, is essential for the progress of humankind as well.

Practice can be seen as an intentional pathway to self-actualisation (à la Aristotle), a conscious choice of freedom (as Sartre might argue), or an inevitable process of becoming (as Heidegger or James might suggest).

However, the one consistent takeaway is that *we are the sum of our actions*, and whether we embrace or avoid practice, it undeniably shapes our future.

So why not aim to be the best versions of ourselves over time?

It's a habit you live every day. So, whatever it is you're after, remember that habits, i.e. your tiny, everyday actions are the architects of your future, who you become & who you are.

Standing On The Shoulder of Giants — Not Oasis But Sir Isaac Newton

"If I have seen further it is by standing on the shoulders of Giants"
— *Sir Isaac Newton*

You've probably heard the quote, "If I have seen further, it is by standing on the shoulders of giants." It's a quote from Sir Isaac Newton, not an Oasis lyric from their album (though Liam Gallagher could probably give it a good spin).

Newton's words cut right to the core of how knowledge, growth, and human progress work. Genius doesn't exist in a vacuum, rather real breakthroughs come from building on what's already there, what others have laid down before you.

It's a humbling yet powerful reminder that we're all part of a much larger continuum. No matter how revolutionary or innovative we think we are, we're always riffing off of what others have done, expanding the conversation that started long before we showed up. Newton, who was arguably one of the brightest minds in history, knew this better than anyone.

The guy literally invented calculus and understood gravity, but he still credited his achievements to the intellectual foundation built by those before him.

There's wisdom in that approach , in that, no one starts from scratch.

The beauty of reading, of learning, is that it's not just information for information's sake. Rather, it's about gaining perspective, letting other people's words and ideas stretch your mind. You don't have to agree with everything. The point is to soak in the ideas, challenge them, and evolve your own thoughts in the process.

Take the works of Descartes, whose *Cogito, ergo sum* ("I think, therefore I am") reshaped Western philosophy by focusing on consciousness itself. Or think of Darwin, whose theory of evolution completely altered our understanding of life and adaptation. By reading these works, we enter into a dialogue with minds of the past, enriching our current understanding with their perspectives.

As a child, I was deeply curious about nature, existence, reality, consciousness, "what is life about?", "why are we here?" & other existential questions, which I could only find in books in the early 90s & 2000s before the treasure trove of the internet opened up. Although times have changed drastically, you can still read & consume books, whether as book summaries on apps or listening to audiobooks.

Reading, acquiring knowledge & learning in this sense, isn't just a passive act. It's a way of learning from the giants who have already blazed trails through the intellectual wilderness before us. Nietzsche once said, "He who would learn to fly one day, must first learn to stand and walk and run and climb and dance; one cannot fly into flying." In other words, before you can innovate or create, you must first familiarise yourself with the existing landscape. You don't reinvent the wheel; you refine it, expand on it, and occasionally, you might even put wings on it.

Descartes, flipped philosophy on its head by focusing on doubt and consciousness. And Nietzsche, who said, "He who has a 'why?' to live can bear almost any how," probed these existential questions. What Nietzsche suggested wasn't about doubt, but about finding meaning through struggle. Both philosophers offer different lenses, but are both equally valuable. By reading their works, you get the full spectrum and you don't have to pick sides. That's the real magic of standing on the shoulders of giants. You gain the wisdom of multiple viewpoints, and you can make better decisions because of it.

Einstein, another giant in his own right, once said, "The more I learn, the more I realise how much I don't know." This comes from a man who redefined our understanding of time and space admitting that his thirst for knowledge only opened up more questions. But that's the point. The search for knowledge isn't about arriving at some ultimate truth, it's about asking better questions and enjoying & partaking in the process of finding the next piece of the puzzle.

When we start to ask: What foundations did Einstein establish? How did he build from Newton? What did Darwin miss? How could Descartes' skepticism apply to AI in today's times?... All these acts of questioning become an intellectual inheritance passed down through generations, evolving just as we have; the living & breathing organisms with the power to think critically & pass down ideas..

This ties directly into the modern habit of continuous learning. Reading isn't just about scanning through the latest self-help book for tips on how to optimise your morning routine (though, it's no shame if that's your jam). It's more about cultivating an intellectual curiosity that makes your mind more adaptable, open, and, well, a bit more giant-like.

Why is this relevant in the modern world? Because life is complex, and so are the problems & dilemmas we face. Whether it's figuring out your next career move, handling relationships, or just trying to make sense of your existence, you're standing on the shoulders of everyone who came before you. They've mapped out certain parts of the landscape, but there are still uncharted territories. Our job is to explore them with their help.

Standing on the shoulders of giants means acknowledging that your work— whether it's in science, art, business, or personal growth—doesn't happen in isolation. You've got to be willing to learn, to read, to engage with ideas that challenge your worldview. The more you know, the more equipped you are to navigate life's complexities.

You're not just standing on the shoulders of giants, in essence, you're becoming one yourself, bit by bit, with each book or essay, article online or body of work you read, each conversation you have, each idea that stretches you beyond your comfort zone.

Be curious & look to expand your curiosity & knowledge.

At the end of the day, Newton's words remind us that knowledge isn't an act of a musician playing solo, it's a concert of a band being beamed down through centuries. It's a relay race, and we're all just passing the baton, building on what's already there, shaping what's to come.

Gaurav Krishnan

The more we read, the more we learn, and the more we contribute to this ever- growing body of collective knowledge. So, if there's any message as important as this—it is to stand tall, read widely, and keep asking those big questions. You never know what heights you'll reach.

Immanuel Kant On Learning & Spreading Knowledge

"Sapere Aude: Dare To Know" — *Immanuel Kant*

When I just transitioned to a career in writing from finance a long time ago, I stumbled upon Immanuel Kant's reflective essay *'What is Enlightenment?'*, which had a significant impact on me. Building on the earlier chapter of learning & acquiring knowledge, which is step one, Immanuel Kant's *What is Enlightenment?* dives deep into the transformative power of **learning first** and **then sharing** knowledge; sharing knowledge being step two.

For Kant, enlightenment is the journey from intellectual passivity to active engagement, a process of thinking for oneself and challenging the comfort of untested ideas. To Kant, true knowledge isn't just about knowing facts; it's about constantly questioning, seeking to understand, and sharing those insights with the world.

Each one of us has a unique perspective that is our own way in which we see the world & what we have learned & experienced from it. So, Kant urges that this knowledge must be responsibly shared via a public medium because you never know who it might impact & who might find it useful. Imagine a world where every one of us kept our thoughts, ideas, and insights locked away.

Where unique perspectives, those specific to our experiences, cultures, and moments of clarity, were left unspoken.

Immanuel Kant, with his essay *What is Enlightenment?* argues against this exact stagnation. For Kant, enlightenment back in his time, wasn't just a matter of intellectual awakening; it was about having the courage to speak your truth in a world that often encouraged silence and conformity.

Kant sees enlightenment as "man's emergence from his self-imposed immaturity or nonage". Immaturity here isn't just naivety but it's when we stop questioning; when we rely entirely on others to tell us what to think or how to live. For Kant, breaking free from this passivity requires both thinking independently and sharing those thoughts, even when they go against the grain.

Why is this important? Because your insights, however specific or personal, could be exactly what someone else needs to hear. It's almost like each of us carries a piece of a much larger puzzle, and that bigger picture only forms when every piece is shared and viewed in light of the whole.

For Kant, "enlightenment" isn't the traditional Eastern notion of "enlightenment," but it is the journey from intellectual passivity to active engagement or a process of thinking for oneself and challenging the comfort of unchartered ideas.

Kant's idea of enlightenment calls for a kind of humility. Your view of the world might be distinct, and yes, even brilliant, but it gains depth only when it meets the perspectives of others. This exchange doesn't dilute your perspective, but in fact, strengthens it. When we share our ideas and genuinely listen to others, our understanding becomes more nuanced, more capable of causing an impact that stands the test of time.

Kant even offers an interesting balance i.e. you don't have to rebel against everything you've been taught. He's not advocating for complete disregard for tradition or authority. Instead, he's saying, question it thoughtfully. Don't let it dictate every action, but don't throw it out either. Respect the wisdom of those who came before, but add your own take.

Think of it like jazz improvisation. The structure of the jazz song is there, on paper, but the beauty of the music only comes out when each musician, each player, adds their unique touch. Kant is urging us to improvise on the notes of human knowledge, to see where we can bring something fresh and innovative to a well-known song.

Kant's call to enlightenment is a call to community; one built not on conformity, but on the richness that comes from genuine diversity of thought. In contributing your perspective, by inviting others to share theirs, you help build a world where knowledge isn't just static. Rather, it's alive, growing, adapting.

And maybe, just maybe, your insight becomes the catalyst for someone else's moment of clarity. For me, it was Joseph Nguyen's book *Don't Believe Everything You Think*.

Your curiosity & pursuit of knowledge should be shared with the collective because of the primary reason that it helps the collective grow. In today's world, the internet is a vast, ever-expanding canvas where our perspectives can reach people across borders and backgrounds.

Through blogs, social media, videos, podcasts and forums, we can share our unique insights and lived experiences, contributing to a global dialogue on everything from personal growth to scientific ideas. Platforms like Medium, Substack, YouTube & Spotify and even other niche forums provide an outlet for voices that, in any other era, might never have been heard outside their local communities.

So maybe we're viewing social media the wrong way. Instead of it just being a place where we share our personal lives, it can be used to share knowledge, experiences, perspective, art, poetry & thought-provoking concepts & ideas. The beauty of sharing this online is that each post, video, or article can resonate with someone unexpectedly and potentially impact their life.

Sometimes, a single tweet or social media post or a blog post can catalyse new perspectives, offering someone clarity, a breakthrough or a sense of belonging. When we put our ideas out there, we invite feedback, build connections, and learn from others in real-time. This exchange enriches the conversation and makes the pursuit of knowledge a collaborative endeavour rather than a solitary pursuit.

Beyond sharing, the internet enables us to mentor, learn, and explore without traditional barriers. It's a landscape where we all have a voice and an audience, and through thoughtful engagement, we can inspire, be inspired, and continually contribute to a more knowledgeable, empathetic, and connected world.

So, get on the online blog or platform and, as Hemmingway writes, "bleed" out your thoughts, ideas & perspective without fear because it could be read or heard by someone somewhere down the line, which they could resonate with & change their lives entirely.

Disruption & Problem Solving

The moments of frustration that work us up, those detours we didn't ask for, are often the very beginnings of innovation. Think about the last time something didn't work the way you expected. Maybe it was a daily inconvenience, like a broken tool or a stubborn system. Most people feel the urge to resist, but what if frustration is actually the spark? A signal for something new?

The story of the *Post-it* note, a classic in invention folklore, comes to mind. What was supposed to be a super-strong adhesive turned out flimsy, but someone noticed its potential. It's a reminder that behind every failure lies a window to rethink the usual way of doing things.

In the face of obstacles, the concept of "creative destruction" makes a case for growth. When you hit a dead end, sometimes the best course is not to fight through but to tear down. That's when real transformation can happen. Rather than simply getting by, it calls for us to dismantle, reimagine, and rebuild with new clarity.

Maybe the most important shift lies in rethinking how we view obstacles themselves. Instead of treating them as barriers, why not see them as invitations to rethink? An invitation to pause, reassess, and move forward with a renewed approach & purpose. Often, what feels like a dead end is simply a prompt to change course.

In his TED Talk *How Frustration Can Make Us More Creative*, Tim Harford presents & explores the idea that unexpected difficulties can actually boost our creativity. Harford shares examples from history like jazz musician Keith Jarrett performing a legendary concert in Cologne, Germany on an untuned piano, to show how obstacles compel us to think differently. Initially, Jarrett refused to play the piano on the night, frustrated with the poor state of the instrument. But when he finally gave in, the limitations of the piano forced Jarrett into uncharted territory, leading to one of the most acclaimed jazz performances ever recorded.

When we encounter challenges, they force us out of autopilot and disrupt our typical problem-solving paths. This cognitive shift, though uncomfortable, drives us to new solutions and insights we may not have reached otherwise.

Harford discusses how psychologists call this the "desirable difficulty" or the idea that frustration and struggle aren't barriers but catalysts. Instead of avoiding discomfort, we should embrace it as a signpost for growth. Just as Jarrett's piano fiasco led to an iconic concert, frustration & roadblocks can unlock hidden levels of resourcefulness in our work and lives.

In his TED Talk, Harford also describes a study involving fonts and learning retention done on a set of college students. Students were given reading material in either a standard, easy-to-read font or a challenging, hard-to-read one. Surprisingly, students who studied the font that was harder to read retained more information & performed better in tests. This "disfluency" effect, where our brains have to work harder to process information, leads to deeper engagement and better recall.

By introducing slight obstacles, like a more difficult font, our minds slow down, engage more thoroughly, and ultimately absorb information better. It's these small disruptions that can sharpen our focus and deepen learning, much like constraints can fuel creativity.

Apart from pioneering ambient music, artist Brian Eno has produced or been involved in a host of successful rock & roll albums over the past 40 years including working with the likes of David Bowie, U2 & Coldplay.

Harford who is a friend of Brian Eno explains how Eno uses a deck of cards called *Oblique Strategies*, which essentially disrupt things in the music studio while recording albums.

Some examples of the cards read:

"Change instrument roles," — which means the drummer sits on the piano, the bass player plays a synth, the guitarist tries the trumpet & so on.

Others read: "Look closely at the most embarrassing details. Amplify them." "Make a sudden, destructive, unpredictable action. Incorporate."

Other prompts like "Use an old idea" or "Try faking it!" challenge conventional thinking, encouraging artists to break out of routine and explore new possibilities.

Despite the session musicians despising these cards, they actually work, and the albums Eno has worked on whether solo or with other artists have all gone platinum.

These "oblique strategies" can be applied to any field of work, and at its core, it's the disruption that creates groundbreaking breakthroughs & newer approaches to tackling professional problems.

So if you're a business owner or in any field of work where you're not seeing enough efficiency & results, or have hit a brick wall while problem-solving, you can try shaking things up with some oblique strategies pertaining to your line of work.

Harford explains that the human brain naturally gravitates towards ease, creating habits to handle most tasks automatically. But creativity often demands a jolt, forcing us to move beyond the comfortable and automatic.

Harford also references the idea of "desirable difficulties" from psychology, noting that obstacles can improve memory and learning by requiring more profound cognitive engagement.

Frustration & disruption, in this sense, become a tool for learning and creativity, reshaping our usual methods and perspectives. So when you hit a brick wall, push through & tear it down & remember, it's a call for reinvention & innovation.

Gaurav Krishnan

Teamwork & Ditching the Limelight

"You only win when you help others win" — *Paul Zen Pilzer*

There's this line in the 2023 film *Oppenheimer* directed by Christopher Nolan where Robert Downey Jr.'s character Lewis Strauss says, "Amateurs seek the sun & get burned, but real power stays in the shadows". However, this isn't about power, this is more to do with cultivating a humble mindset through our actions and while working in teams.

Today we're familiar with the names Neil Armstrong and Buzz Aldrin. They're, after all, the first human beings to set foot on the moon, "One small step for man, one giant leap for mankind," the iconic words said by Armstrong as he walked on the surface of the moon, remain legendary and inspirational to people across the world to this day.

However, there was another crew member on the Apollo 11 mission to the moon, of whom people are perhaps unaware. His name was Michael Collins. Collins piloted the Apollo 11 and circled the moon 26 times until Armstrong and Aldrin finished their work on the moon's surface and got them safely back onboard the spacecraft and piloted them back to Earth.

Collins went all the way up there, within touching distance of the moon and didn't set foot on the surface & left that feat for only Armstrong and Aldrin.

When the team returned back to Earth and both Armstrong and Aldrin were in the spotlight & swarmed by the media, Collins took a step back and remained unperturbed & unphased. He let his crew members enjoy the spotlight and was content with his role on the Apollo 11 mission. Despite being an integral component of the success of the historic mission, after all, he was the pilot, Collins let his crew members shine and take the spotlight, while he sat back and remained content without the recognition or fame.

Collins, in essence, ditched the limelight & let others win & stayed humble despite his great feat; he was part of a team on a historic mission and was a pivotal part of the Apollo 11 crew, however, after they returned to Earth, Collins told the media that he was perfectly happy occupying one of those three seats on the Apollo 11. Collins was clear about his definition of success (as I've explained in the earlier chapter) and he created value and offered his skills and expertise in being the third yet integral crew member of the Apollo 11 mission.

Collins helped his team members shine and didn't hog or immerse himself in the glory and fame of the spotlight. He let his team members win and in doing so, became a success.

Another story much akin to Collins is that of a Spanish football player named Jose Maria Gutierrez Hernandez or simply—Guti.

Guti was a Real Madrid youth academy graduate who made his way up to the first team at the Santiago Bernabeu. This was a time when Real Madrid were called the *Galacticos* because of the star names they had in their squad: the likes of Ronaldo Nazario, Raul, Zidane, Figo, Beckham etc.

However, Guti would prove to be a pivotal figure in Real Madrid's success during those years by simply being the 'provider' and main creative midfielder.

Guti was an intelligent & cerebral midfielder, and some of his assists are simply genius. Guti was happy to provide assists to his teammates, at times even when he was 1v1 with the goalkeeper. There's one particular assist where he's 1 v 1 with the goalie and backheels the ball back to his teammate for him to score.

Unselfish and positionally aware, Guti would become the top assist provider during the *Galacticos* era, and surrounded by stars in the squad, Guti would let them shine and take the spotlight, as he went about his game with minimal fuss but at the same time being an important member of the team.

Guti's assists are now part of folklore at Real Madrid and he amassed a total of 107 assists in his time at the Madrid club winning 3 UEFA Champions League titles and 5 La Liga titles. Guti captained Real Madrid on several occasions, and was given the armband not just because he was an academy player but because of his unselfishness and exemplary ability to combine with his teammates.

Another example could be that of music producer Nigel Godrich, the main brains behind the production of the mercurial alternative rock band Radiohead's music.

Godrich, was a key figure in Radiohead achieving their world-renowned and highly celebrated sound. While band members Thom Yorke and guitarist Jonny Greenwood are the main creative driving forces of Radiohead's sound, and share much of the spotlight, Godrich's work behind the scenes and in turning the songs into a finished product, is exemplary and commendable.

To put it into context, Radiohead wouldn't have achieved their desired sound without Godrich's production capabilities as a music producer and sound engineer.

In the music business, producers often play a pivotal role, but remain in the wings and work behind the scenes. While the band or artist gets the credit and accolades for their music, a music producer's work is integral and considerably important, although it doesn't feature in the limelight.

So, at certain instances and throughout our personal and professional work life, there are times when we have to help our team win, or others win, without the fame and glory for ourselves.

Working in a team means that you have to sacrifice the personal for the collective and it's perhaps better in some instances that you're not in the spotlight.

Doing your duty & doing your best behind the scenes and contributing to the overall success of a team, without the fuss and glamour of the spotlight, working silently and diligently to show your team your worth, skill and expertise, is another way to create value and be an integral cog in achieving a team goal.

Make Your Own Waves

To the outside world it might not seem important but to your team and the people you are making win; the value of you and your work will be appreciated considerably.

So, it really doesn't matter whether you're in the spotlight or get the fame for your work or not, you can be a success by helping others win.

It might seem counterintuitive but it's not just about you; help others win and subsequently win too — it's a hallmark of working in a team.

Some Drugs Help Explore What's Within, Make It An Experience Not A Habit

Take me back to 2010 or 2011 & I can tell you plenty of stories about doing drugs; it depends on how bored you are. But bland humour & cantor aside, it was a blurry yet meaningful few years taking drugs — years that have now evaporated as quickly as the smoke trails from a spliff or chillum (an Indian hash pipe).

We were midway through college when the drugs took over. It was a scene. My regular weekend would be to wake up & smoke a few joints with my roommates in our penthouse apartment in the morning, whether it was a 'tee' or 'tola' of Himalayan hashish or Manipal's customary marijuana. Occasionally when the heavier stoners were around, it would result in a chillum being passed around. Make it to lunch & classes which were followed by evening drinks & my regular stint as the DJ of the most happening pub in town. We'd eventually stagger our way back to the apartment & hit the mighty ol' bong which we named "James Bong", heading way into the far reaches of the night.

But as the pot gave way to the need for something more, LSD became something that gripped our batch at around the turn of 2010 giving way to 2011. A few groups began to take acid at a few parties in Goa & soon a large chunk of our batch wanted to drop too. My flatmates & I ventured into the unknown & the realms of acid in the summer of 2011. It was May & our semester had just completed; we stuck around & headed to Goa & then Gokarna to drop our first few blotters & then a trip to Kodaikanal for magic mushrooms.

Make Your Own Waves

The surreality of the experience aside, acid & shrooms were rather eye-opening in different ways in hindsight. To just view reality blur & bounce & shape & form & flow — ah, I could go on — but to view those stunning visuals & feel music, not just listen, but feel music through my body, it was something I had never comprehended until then. Given my penchant for theoretical physics, my trip was a lot about what I would see visually on the drugs staring into the vastness of the sky & then about individuality, feeling this ball of energy in the centre of my chest & of course, music.

Drugs can be used as a "gateway" as explained by comedian George Carlin; they help you tap into what's inside yourself. Creativity soaring on pot or finding purpose & meaning after LSD or mushrooms, drugs can help us connect with our inner selves. But of course, there's the other side of drug use — the addiction side — which can get pretty ugly.

Drugs should be just an experience, not a habit. If you're up for the journey & the experience you could try drugs at some point in your life. Trying some LSD or shrooms or micro dosing has a plethora of benefits & it's just so staggering visually. It could also lead to significant breakthroughs & explorations of the inner workings of your mind & consciousness, but ensure that you do so responsibly & after doing your research.

It can be a beautiful experience that could help propel your life into a new direction & help you gain more perspective or even heal. But be careful with how you use them, and how much you use them. Make it only a one-off experience as compared to something regular and try to go deeper within yourself & just perceive and experience the surreal moments on those substances. Essentially, drugs aren't an evil; they're just another experience.

Gaurav Krishnan

Connect The Dots: The Steve Jobs Perspective

"You have to connect the dots. You can't connect the dots looking forward; you can only connect them looking backwards. So you have to trust that the dots will somehow connect in your future. You have to trust in something—your gut, destiny, life, karma, whatever. This approach has never let me down, and it has made all the difference in my life."
- Steve Jobs

Steve Jobs needs no introduction. His visionary work with founding Apple & his reinvention with Pixar and all his life's work has created unbelievable value for people around the globe.

In his speech to Stanford graduates, Jobs delivered a very interesting perspective about what he calls, "connecting the dots".

Jobs suggests that all that you've experienced or studied in school and university, and excelled at, or were interested in, will eventually come of some use in your life as you grow older and that you just have to believe that it will. This includes what you're drawn towards as a child and your passions, jobs, and subjects you've studied in your teens and then your twenties.

Jobs says that these are dots on the map for mapping your future, and he further elaborates that you can only connect the dots looking backwards and not forwards.

When Jobs dropped out of college, he would attend random classes based on his interests and one such class he took was a calligraphy class. As time progressed and after Jobs founded Apple, those lessons he learned in calligraphy class became the basis for the design of the computer keyboard that we know today and use universally.

Make Your Own Waves

It's staggering to just think that a simple class Jobs took for kicks, became the model for the computer keyboard that is now a worldwide standard!

This is a prime example that Jobs' connecting the dots philosophy does hold good. If Jobs hadn't taken that calligraphy class, we wouldn't have the modern- day keyboard designed in the way it is today.

Looking back on my life and connecting the dots in my life, music, football, film, writing & learning programming have been the biggest dots that I've connected that just fell into place in my younger years, which have come of use to me today.

So what have been the dots in your life?

Can you think of what you were naturally drawn towards in your childhood?

What subjects were you more inclined towards and which were the subjects that you excelled at in school?

What did you study for your under graduation degree? What were the courses you took during university?

What were your first few jobs about and which industry & sector were they in? What were some of your most vivid and loved experiences in the past?

How do they align with your passions?

Look back on your life, contemplate what your dots were and begin to write them down and connect them to your current life. They'll often be linked to your future purpose.

Even a random course or subject you took in university could come of use and spark something new in your life and guide you towards your future, just like it did for Steve Jobs.

So take out a book and a pen, look back & note down what you think your dots are, and connect them to your current life & who knows, you could engineer something, create something or pursue something that excites you.

In turn, it could lead to something you'd love to do which will enable you to create and explore your passions on a deeper level.

Live Below Your Means, Be Humble & Don't Be A Victim of Consumerism

"Advertising has us chasing cars and clothes, working jobs we hate so we can buy shit we don't need. We're the middle children of the history man, no purpose or place, we have no Great war, no Great depression, our great war is a spiritual war, our great depression is our lives, we've been all raised by television to believe that one day we'd all be millionaires and movie gods and rock stars, but we won't, and we're slowly learning that fact, and we're very very pissed off." - Tyler Durden (Fight Club by Chuck Palahniuk)

This is a quote by Tyler Durden, the fictional character in the movie *Fight Club* based on the book of the same name by Chuck Palahniuk.

There are parts of this quote I agree with and parts I don't. It's certain that consumerism has been on the rise ever since the invention of the television and perhaps, even before that. Consumerism makes us all dopamine & trigger happy — buy the next dress, by the next piece of furniture, buy the next car, buy this sh*t, buy that; all advertising does is shove products & services up our throats, because companies want you to click and buy & subscribe to sh*t.

The white collar job, the invention of the 20th century, began this vicious cycle which then morphed into hyper consumerism in the 21st century along with the desire to constantly consume like a conveyor belt from hell. We've all been there, the need for more products and more material goods that give us a hit of dopamine.

In this world derided with constant consumption, it's up to use to filter out what we actually need, and what we don't.

In today's hyper-consumerist landscape, the advice to "live below your means" holds more significance than ever. It's a message that's often overshadowed by the allure of acquiring more, yet figures like Ratan Tata and Warren Buffet stand as living testaments to its power.

Ratan Tata, the late celebrated former chairman of the Tata Group, exemplified humility and a lifestyle that contrasts sharply with modern consumerist pressures.

Despite leading one of India's largest conglomerates, Tata was known for living a remarkably modest life. He famously avoided luxury, drove himself in a Tata car, and preferred understated clothing. Even during his leadership of the Tata Group, he was often seen eating in the company's cafeteria alongside employees, keeping a level of simplicity and approachability that set him apart in corporate India

This mindset reflects a deeply embedded principle in Tata's approach to leadership and life. Living below one's means is not just about financial prudence but about embracing values of humility, moderation, and social responsibility. For instance, when Tata orchestrated the acquisitions of international brands like Jaguar, Land Rover and Corus Steel, he prioritised sustainable and ethical growth, understanding that wealth and power should also serve society.

Over 60% of the Tata Group's profits have consistently been directed to education, healthcare, and social welfare through the Tata Trusts, demonstrating his commitment to philanthropy and social impact.

Similarly, Warren Buffet, one of the wealthiest individuals globally, has lived in the same house for decades, one he bought long before he became a billionaire. Buffet's habits emphasise that wealth isn't about amassing possessions but understanding where to invest your time, energy, and money.

He frequently warns against "lifestyle inflation," where each pay raise or success tempts you into greater and often unnecessary spending. For him, real wealth means peace of mind and the freedom that comes from smart financial choices rather than flashy acquisitions.

It's not just about saving money, it's about saving yourself from the clutches of a constant need & the greed for more. Instead you can be happy & live freely & with humility without the need for constantly acquiring more possessions.

Tackling consumerism in today's context can be particularly challenging, with constant digital prompts and ads encouraging endless upgrading and accumulation. However, Ratan Tata's example, alongside those of leaders like Warren Buffet, who also advocates for a frugal, principle-driven lifestyle, offers a compelling alternative to this consumerist cycle.

Choosing to focus on intrinsic fulfilment and mindful spending, as both men exemplify, encourages a life rich in purpose & experience rather than possessions.

By questioning the necessity of every purchase and placing value on experiences like travel, or empowering ones like education, and community well-being over material gain, we can resist consumerism and instead lead lives focused on lasting significance.

So, how do we tackle consumerism in an era driven by constant ads on the internet, peer pressure, and a "newest is best" mentality?

First, consider what truly adds value to your life. Are purchases filling a need or simply an impulse? Take a moment to pause before the next online splurge; there's power in restraint. Mindful consumerism i.e. prioritising quality over quantity, opting for long-term rather than short-term fulfilment is a personal choice and a powerful one.

Instead of succumbing to every trend, you can choose a more measured approach, focusing on essentials that enhance your life without draining your finances or cluttering your space. Of course you can spend on something you really want impulsively occasionally, but it's key to not make it a habit.

When we live below our means, we create a buffer for ourselves. Essentially, it's a safety net that keeps us stable during life's ups and downs & it's more about staying true to yourself & living in a humble manner acknowledging your journey through life & how every human being has their share of struggles. This safety net perhaps came to the fore during the COVID pandemic.

Financial stability & living humbly while not being swayed by consumerism allows us to be in control rather than feeling tethered to debt or a lifestyle that's more aspirational than sustainable.

In the end, humility and simplicity can be the ultimate forms of freedom.

You can find a more detailed article on consumerism on my Medium...

Gaurav Krishnan

The Road Less Traveled Robert Frost's Poem

"I shall be telling this with a sigh
Somewhere ages and ages hence:
Two roads diverged in a wood, and I—
I took the one less travelled by,
And that has made all the difference."
- Robert Frost

In the quiet expanse of a yellow wood, Robert Frost's narrator stands at a fork, observing two diverging paths. The choice before him is less about practicality and more about the courage to choose differently. Frost's *The Road Not Taken* is a poem for the lone travellers and curious minds who, by design or defiance, opt for the road less wandered. And while this "less travelled" road may be daunting, the rewards of choosing it often lie not in the destination but in the act of diverging.

Frost's poem offers a timeless image of being willing to explore where few dare to go. "I took the one less travelled by, and that has made all the difference." It's an ode to the kind of visionaries who resist conventional maps in favour of something entirely unique. It's a rather simple image that taps into something universal, the urge to choose our own way, knowing that choice itself shapes us. It's more than just picking a road; it's about creating a life that is not just different from the consensus but feels real, impactful, and unapologetically ours.

Frost's narrator, standing in front of the two paths, takes the "one less traveled by," that reflects a conscious decision to veer from the commonly taken path, perhaps to risk the unconventional for something more profound. And it's this notion of embracing the "road less travelled" that underpins some of history's most impactful figures.But in this chapter, I'll take a look at the lives of hedge fund pioneer Jim Simons & his hedge fund Renaissance Technologies and the Renaissance philosopher Michel de Montaigne.

Jim Simons is a modern-day example of someone who chose the road less travelled, both literally and intellectually. Simons, who started Renaissance Technologies, a wildly successful hedge fund, wasn't your average Wall Street trader. He was a former math professor who entered the world of finance with zero background in economics, business acumen or traditional trading.

Simons didn't follow the norms or the playbook of typical investors. Instead, he gathered a team of mathematicians, scientists, and cryptographers—people who didn't fit the Wall Street mould—and developed sophisticated algorithms to guide his trades. This was decades before computers & quant strategies for trading were used, significantly aeons before they became a mainstream concept. Simons' strategy, relying on quantitative models and massive data sets, was so radically different from the norm at the time that few could understand or replicate his success.

Simons gathered a team as diverse as his vision including cryptographers, physicists, and computer scientists, crafting complex algorithms that made his hedge fund wildly successful. In choosing this unconventional path, Simons created financial success, and he reinvented what a hedge fund could be. His decision to seek solutions in science and mathematics and statistics rather than finance reflects a critical point of Frost's poem that it's often the unpaved road, and the counter-intuitive direction, that reveals the most profound discoveries.

At the heart of Simons' story lies his mindset to go against the grain. Like Frost's poem, Simons made a conscious choice to tread where few dared, ultimately reaping the rewards of a path that most didn't even know existed.

Instead of asking, "What is everyone else doing?" Simons and his team were constantly asking, "What's a different way to approach this?" & "How can I do things differently from everyone else?". His success lies in his willingness to walk a road not defined by others' expectations or norms, a concept central to Frost's message.

Turning the clock back to the Renaissance period, Michel de Montaigne, the French Renaissance philosopher, similarly embraced a path of intellectual independence. Living in a time marked by rigid societal structures, Montaigne pioneered the modern essay as a means of self-inquiry, deliberately avoiding dogma and easy answers.

Montaigne wrote to discover and to explore ideas from all angles rather than to impose conclusions. He trusted his internal dialogue over popular opinion, carving out a unique place in literature and philosophy that has endured for centuries. Montaigne's philosophy underscores the idea that introspection and the courage to explore unorthodox beliefs are, in themselves, a path worth taking.

Montaigne's life was marred with loss & hardship. His only true friend, Étienne de La Boétie, died in 1563 at a young age, an event that devastated Montaigne.

Family life also brought Montaigne profound sorrows. Of his six children, only one daughter, Léonor, survived into adulthood. The repeated deaths of his young children weighed heavily on him, and in his writings, he frequently alluded to the pain of parental loss. This exposure to death and suffering led Montaigne to confront the human condition head-on, fuelling his reflections on mortality, acceptance, and the importance of living with awareness of the fleeting nature of life..

In his works, Montaigne stressed on the importance of following your own path & his work was unapologetically unique & free "of artifice & pretence", as he put it.

Living in a turbulent 16th-century France, Montaigne diverged from the scholastic tradition and the rigorous structures of philosophy, instead producing writings that were deeply personal and introspective. Rather than attempting to dictate universal truths or provide moral instruction, which most philosophers were doing at the time, he explored his inner life, documenting his thoughts, emotions, and observations about humanity in a candid, almost confessional style of writing.

Montaigne famously described his work as "an attempt," reflecting his belief that philosophy should reflect personal experience and uncertainty rather than authoritative doctrine.

Make Your Own Waves

One of Montaigne's most defining traits was his willingness to question norms, underpinning the importance of self-inquiry and embracing an unfiltered look at one's own experience. This approach can be seen in his essay *On the Education of Children,* where he argued that education should cultivate individual judgment rather than conform to obedience, and in *On Cannibals,* he challenges European ethnocentrism by contrasting it with the practices of indigenous cultures.

Montaigne's call to follow one's own path aligned with the classical Greek exhortation to "know thyself." He was influenced by Stoic and Skeptic philosophies, both of which explore detachment and introspection as pathways to wisdom.

However, unlike many philosophers of his time, Montaigne believed that embracing one's contradictions and uncertainties was essential. He often explored both sides of an argument, allowing readers to see the complexities of each issue and challenging them to arrive at their own conclusions.

His essay *That to Philosophise is to Learn How to Die* tackles the fear of death and the ways in which facing mortality can shape the way one lives, encouraging individuals to confront life's inherent uncertainty with courage and honesty.

Montaigne's work was revolutionary for its time, prioritising personal insight and self-reflection in an era dominated by religious and political dogma. In examining his own thoughts and admitting his doubts and vulnerabilities, he set a new standard for intellectual honesty, which influenced philosophers like Blaise Pascal, Friedrich Nietzsche, and even Ralph Waldo Emerson centuries later.

Why Montaigne's stance is important is because he went against the usual kind of writing of his time, and focussed his work on his own experiences & in trying to understand & put words to his own life & his self, urging following your own path & making sense of your own life.

Montaigne's essays invite readers to question the world and themselves, making his work a timeless call to intellectual freedom and self-expression. While delving into personal experience over collective dogma, Montaigne encouraged generations of thinkers to honour their own perspectives, forge their own paths, and seek understanding not through conformity but through individuality.

The beauty of Frost's poem *The Road Not Taken* isn't in its message to abandon everything familiar but in its invitation to choose wisely, even when that choice goes against popular notion. The poem offers us an understanding that to be a pioneer, whether in our personal lives or on a grander scale, we must sometimes choose the harder path, the quieter path, the one that allows us to engage deeply with our values and desires rather than merely accepting the world as it is.

So perhaps, standing at your own crossroads, take a moment to consider Frost's simplistic yet profound exploration of the road less travelled. Take inspiration from the lives of Simons and Montaigne, and remind yourself that the most fulfilling paths are often the ones that others overlook.

Taking the road less travelled often allows us to not only find ourselves but also leave a legacy for others. The journey may be uncertain, but as Frost knew well, it's this very act of choosing that makes all the difference.

Invent Yourself, & Keep Reinventing Yourself

"Invent yourself and then reinvent yourself," wrote Charles Bukowski in his poem *No Leaders Please*, a fierce rebuke and anthem urging self-creation & reinvention. "Change your tone and shape so often that they can never categorise you," he suggested, implying that the journey of self-invention and reinvention emerges as a cornerstone of independence and a rebellion against stagnation.

Bukowski's voice is raw, and unapologetically real & speaks about the necessity of shaping and reshaping ourselves continuously, not waiting for permission or validation from society. In a world that seems to want us conforming, categorised, and packaged, the act of creating yourself anew becomes an art of adaptability & building on Robert Frost's poem in the last chapter, your unique path.

In his TED Talk, *You Don't Actually Know What Your Future Self Wants*, Shankar Vedantam explains that most of us are terrible at predicting our future desires and avenues, often clinging to our present identities as if they were immutable. Vedantam's concept of the "end of history illusion" explores how we tend to see ourselves as static, mistakenly believing that we have finished evolving. But, in reality, the self & its evolution is in constant flux. This means that in order to meet our future selves, we must embrace reinvention as a way of life.

The concept of the "end of history illusion," is a psychological phenomenon where we underestimate how much we will change over time. He explains that we tend to view our present selves as relatively fixed, often failing to anticipate that our preferences, values, and even personalities will continue to evolve.

We look back and see how much we've changed but believe that now, finally, we have reached our "true" self. Vedantam points out that years later, we look back on the current self in the same way—as just another step in a continuous evolution. This illusion can lead us to make decisions that our future selves might find baffling or unsatisfactory because we're basing choices on **who we are today** rather than based on **who we might become.**

One of the most interesting aspects Vedantam touches on is the impact this illusion has on our decision-making and, ultimately, on our happiness. If we don't anticipate our future growth, we may make commitments that feel right in the moment but can later seem constraining. Vedantam further warns that this often leads to regret, as our future selves grow into new perspectives and aspirations that no longer align with our earlier choices.

This tendency can keep us from taking on new challenges, exploring unknown territories, or even questioning our current paths. The essence of Vedantam's message ties directly to the theme of continual self-reinvention. If we stay fixed in the belief that we've "arrived" at our final selves, we miss opportunities for transformation, opportunities that the likes of artists, thinkers, and innovators leverage to break new ground.

In music, few bands embody this concept better than Radiohead, who have sculpted their niche style & sound in perpetual self-reinvention. Their 1997 album *OK Computer* placed them at the pinnacle of rock music, adored by fans and critics alike, the album was heralded as a cornerstone of late 90s music given its alternative-rock sound & theme. It could have been the end goal & final sound, the peak, perhaps. But the band turned away from their sound & style on *OK Computer* to disrupt it in their next release. With their 2000 album *Kid A*, they swerved into unchartered territory with experimental electronic sounds, breaking away from expectations and redefining what a rock album could be.

Their subsequent release *In Rainbows* sound-wise, was the band coming full circle, finally finding a balance between their old & new styles of electronic & rock soundscapes, merging rock and roll with electronic influences & approaches to create what was arguably their best & most critically acclaimed album. With *In Rainbows*, they reimagined distribution models as well, releasing it on a pay-what-you-want basis, inviting their audience to buy their album at whatever price they felt like. Then with 2011's *The King of Limbs*, they stripped their sound down to minimalism and rhythm, exploring new territories yet again. While 2016's *A Moon Shaped Pool* explored disillusionment & a mishmash of soundscapes from stripped down pianos & acoustic guitars & a more wholesome sound drawing from their previous two releases.

For Radiohead, reinvention was never one-dimensional but a commitment to exploring new sounds and ideas that resonated with them & their ideas of innovation.

What ties these varied acts of reinvention together, whether it's Bukowski's searing imploration, Vedantam's psychological insights, or Radiohead's artistic evolution is a dedication to the notion that we are almost always a work in progress. Reinvention is a way of staying true to ourselves by shedding skins that no longer fit, a process of peeling back layers to reach something raw, unexpected, and essential.

We need to keep reinventing ourselves asreinvention keeps us adaptable, especially as the world changes faster than we can predict.

Reinvention is more than a choice: it's essential for personal growth, societal progress, and innovation. At its core, reinvention helps us adapt to new circumstances, respond to shifting needs, and redefine success on our own terms. This continual transformation whether in our personal lives or as a society propels us forward, helping us stay resilient and dynamic in an ever- changing world.

Reinventing ourselves can take many forms, whether it's in our careers, relationships, or lifestyles. Each area offers unique opportunities to break away from old patterns and embrace growth. Here are just some examples:

Career

Consider changing industries, learning new skills, or launching a side project to explore different passions. Online courses and networking are invaluable resources to ease the transition, allowing you to test the waters before a full career shift.

Relationships

Strengthening relationships may mean setting healthier boundaries, nurturing more intentional connections, or letting go of connections that no longer align with ourselves & our growth. Practising open communication and empathy can help form lasting, fulfilling relationships.

Lifestyle

Small lifestyle changes, like simplifying belongings & living minimalistically, practising gratitude, or relocating like moving closer to nature for a slower pace of life or to a new city for a fresh cultural experience, can profoundly influence your day-to-day well-being. Even incremental shifts, like integrating eco-friendly practices, can reshape how we experience life.

Mindset

Adopting a growth mindset lets you view challenges as learning opportunities. Self-reflection and mindfulness help identify self-limiting beliefs, creating a mental foundation for reinvention. As suggested by psychologist Carol Dweck, we can shift from fixed views of success to seeing every experience as an opportunity for learning & finding joy & satisfaction in the small incremental gains & the small joys of life to in turn, find more fulfilment.

Health & Wellness

New health routines, whether it's exploring a different form of exercise, nutrition, or setting digital detoxes, can revitalise both physical and mental well-being. This could mean changing your approach to exercise by embracing practices like running, yoga or hiking instead of the traditional gym routine. Focusing on wellness might also involve setting regular digital detoxes, promoting mental clarity and reducing stress.

Creativity

Creativity enhances self-expression. Trying new forms of art, music, or writing can unlock fresh perspectives, bringing innovation to all parts of life. Whether it's learning to play an instrument, painting, writing, or even trying a new dance style, creative pursuits unlock new dimensions of self-expression. As explored in the earlier chapter, engaging with the arts taps into deeper emotions and can offer a profound sense of renewal.

Spirituality & Philosophy

Reading about & exploring new philosophies or spiritual practices can foster deeper self-understanding, helping clarify values and life direction. Whether you explore Eastern philosophies, like Buddhism or Taoism, or Western thinkers like Kierkegaard or Nietzsche, or Western thinkers influenced by Eastern thought like Alan Watts, Eckhart Tolle, or others, philosophy allows us to explore life's biggest questions. These new perspectives offer clarity on our values, purpose, and direction, shaping the foundation of our personal evolution.

In essence, reinvention is a gradual yet powerful journey of small shifts & step by step increments in our lives that, together, create a path toward a more fulfilled and purposeful life.

Gaurav Krishnan

The Reward Is To Play & Mushin — The Flow State

You've probably heard quotes like "the journey is the destination", or "joy is found not in finishing an activity, but in doing it", but at their core, they're very true statements. In their book *The Courage To Be Disliked*, authors Ichiro Kishimi & Fumitake Koga suggest that, "We must take pride in the here and now; the present. We might be aiming for a goal, but we need to appreciate the little gifts life has granted us while we wait. Without this, we might lose focus on the essential things. The goal is important, but so is the journey to it. If we are too focused on the future, we risk ever living in the now."

As a musician or artist, you often get lost in the before & after while you're making music, or any kind of art for that matter. You know stuff in the after phase like, "Will people like it?", "Will my music get 'x' streams?", "Will this song get onto a lot of playlists?", "Will some music media company write a piece about my music?", "Will I get signed onto a label?" etc.

Meanwhile, when you're just approaching a song or track or are in the middle of it, your mind will spin into those chasms of questions & second-guessing, "Will this riff, lick, motif or sample work?", "Will this sample/motif sound better than this other one", "Does this sound good?" "Should I change this section or that?", "Should I revise my approach?", and so on & so forth.

If you've ever picked up a musical instrument or endeavoured to create music or art, it's a long-term tryst; almost a lifelong journey. Every time you pick up an instrument, there's a new sound, there's a new scale, a new chord progression, a new lick, a new song, the constant need to experiment & desire to improve at it— but it's the **process** that is at the heart of the journey.

We've all been there. Chances are if you're engaged in any art form — music, film, writing, painting or sketching, anything — the proverbial gauntlet of how it's received and the end results hang down on the creative's soul proliferating the genuine process & the enjoyment of creating it in the first place.

Like Alan Watts says, "This is the real secret of life — to be completely engaged with what you are doing in the here and now. And instead of calling it work, realise it is play."

Whether you indulge in or like quotes & reflect on them or not, all you have in the end while living life is the **journey** — the **process**.

Life is like a jazz improvisation or a free-form jam session; it thrives in moments that cannot be precisely scripted or planned. Life almost becomes its own art form, a **process** without a definitive, polished end; it's more of a rhythm than a roadmap.

There's a freedom in this way of living, i.e. by enjoying the process of life like the process of playing an instrument. It's a call for us to stay present, to show up fully, and to embrace each choice along the way. This theme isn't new; it weaves throughout history in many forms. To the ancient Greeks, the value of life lay not in the length of days but in their richness. It was about the depth of each experience, each connection, and each challenge that moulded them.

Sometimes, though, the messy parts of life feel more like a mistake than music. If we take a cue from jazz musicians—legends like John Coltrane or Miles Davis—we learn that errors can be reworked, & turned into something rich and unexpected. It's like finding the harmony in dissonance. Every missed note is just another step toward the song's true form; life's unpredictability isn't a hurdle but a process. When we're willing to engage with the mess, each stumble becomes a part of our growth.

Musicians often talk about *finding flow*, a state where they lose themselves in the music, feeling time dissolve. That's the Japanese concept of *Mushin*.

So where does *Mushin* come in?

Mu (無) is nothing or nothingness, and shin (心) refers to the mind.

"*Mushin* is the mind of no-mind." The 'non-thinking' state of 'flow' is called *Mushin*. It happens when we're totally engrossed in doing certain things.

Sportspersons also experience *Mushin* when they're totally 'in the zone' or 'in the pocket' & are playing at their peak. Being a Japanese samurai philosophy as well, it also relates to combat. Whether it's in sports, combat or music, — the next pass, the next punch, the next note, all happen in the state of *Mushin*.

In his book *Don't Believe Everything You Think* the author Joseph Nguyen extends *Mushin* to relating it to our goals & ambitions by delightfully bracketing our goals, targets & ambitions into two buckets, i.e. goals created out of **desperation** & goals created out of **inspiration.**

He suggests that where the goals come from determine their nature.

Goals created out of **desperation** are usually because **we want something out of them** & make us feel daunted, stressed out & anxious. We feel scarcity, urgency, heavy & like they're a burden. Self doubt seeps in & we feel a constant lack of worth if we don't achieve them.

Goals set in the state of desperation are **needs** goals and not **ends** goals. We set the goal to accomplish something else.

For example starting a business to make sufficiently enough income so that we have financial freedom, or working that extra bit to make more money or tutoring or teaching to make more money on the side or doing anything because you want something out of it. We feel like we **have** to do these things & not **want** to do them.

Paradoxically, even after we achieve the goal, we eventually return back to the same feelings of lack of worth & feeling more empty & wanting more, just as the chapter on Schopenhauer's thought reveals.

Goals set out of **inspiration**, on the other hand, are born out of *Mushin* & **make you feel like they're a calling**, you feel expansive & deeply moved & inspired. Instead of feeling like they're an obligation **you feel compelled to do them.**

"In this state we are creating because we feel deeply moved…. it feels like there's a powerful force of life coming from within us…. This is why painters paint, writers write, dancers dance, singers sing, even if they never get paid or make a living from it. When you feel pulled by a force to create something you gravitate towards it, you feel compelled to do it. When you feel like this, you're creating from a place of abundance not lack." Nguyen says.

Goals from this state are because we **want to** & not **have to**. Not for any other reason.

"This feeling of deep inspiration…. comes from something greater than us. I'd like to call it 'divine inspiration'," he adds.

It's an expansive state & we feel whole, fulfilled & brimming with abundance & we don't judge, compare, rationalise & it doesn't get diluted by thinking.

Everyone experiences this in their lives. Think about all the moments in your life you felt divine inspiration when it felt like it was a calling. When you did something, you truly wanted to & were inspired to do it. It doesn't matter whether you actually created something or not. But rather, what it was & how you felt. It comes from the state of *Mushin*.

Of course, the world elicits the need for both kinds of goals — money being the end target for a desperate goal & divine inspiration seeping in for an inspired goal. It's not good or bad if you have majorly desperate goals, after all the bills need to be paid & everybody wants financial freedom but the ideal way is to balance them & oscillate between them i.e. goals born out of desperation and goals born out of inspiration.

The practicality of thinking & life & just the way the world is, entails the need to achieve desperate goals but balancing them with more inspired goals can lead to more fulfilment. In some cases, especially for creative people, their inspired goals can also lead to that old' gravy train of money. However, it's all about balance.

A writer I follow named Maria Popova often writes about the importance of staying attentive to life's minutiae—those smaller rhythms that build the "song" of our days. For example, even routine activities can bring fulfilment, whether it's cooking, gardening, or exercising.

Each small action becomes part of the grander rhythm of our life, reminding us that the act of "playing" the notes in life's grand musical gig makes the journey & songs more memorable, regardless of external reception or applause (the end result).

Ultimately, the reward is not in the final product but in the ongoing, evolving, imperfect *experience of living*. It's also necessary to enjoy the process of achieving your goals & targets. By engaging fully with life—taking in the messy, unpredictable, and beauty of the process—we discover that the act of "playing" is a reward in itself & furthermore, the act of 'playing' is where life truly unfolds.

In essence, life is like playing an instrument, in that *the reward is to play*. Not the stuff that comes before or after. The process of living, the act of play, is the grandest reward of life. It makes our days worthwhile, gives us meaning and solace and just like playing an instrument, it gives us the feeling of fulfilment, all encompassed in the grand & beautiful act of living or the act of playing.

Essentially, we must learn to appreciate the *process*, the process of living life, and not just the goals or end results. We ultimately realise that *the reward is to play* and not just the end results that come and go. So immerse yourself in the process of living and appreciate life's journey, because it's in the process of *playing* and *living* that our 4000 weeks ultimately unfold.

Family & Relationships Keep Us Happy & Healthy

What truly makes for a long, fulfilling, and healthy life? The answer isn't found in wealth or career milestones, nor is it simply about gym routines or a flawless diet & wellness. It's something more fundamental, interwoven into our very existence as human beings: relationships.

In 1938, Harvard set out on a remarkable journey to understand the key to what made a long, healthy life by following the lives of 724 young men from two vastly different backgrounds. One group comprised Harvard sophomores, chosen for their intelligence and privileged backgrounds. While the other group came from Boston's poorest neighbourhoods, who came from upbringing shaped by struggle and scarcity.

For more than 75 years, these men were tracked through countless interviews, medical exams, and in-depth surveys, making this study the longest and most comprehensive on adult development and longevity in history. Astonishingly, the findings didn't point to wealth, education, or success as predictors of a fulfilling and long life. Instead, it all boiled down to the power of relationships.

So, what does this mean? The Harvard study surfaced three core lessons on relationships and well-being that apply universally:

1. Social connections are really good for us and loneliness kills

The study showed that people who are more socially connected to family, friends and community are happier, healthier and live longer than people who are less connected. Loneliness proves toxic. The people who are more isolated from others find that they are less happy, their health declines earlier in midlife and they live shorter lives. Furthermore, isolation was found to be a harbinger of earlier declines in health in most cases.

2. It's not the quantity but the quality of our close relationships that matter

Living in the midst of conflict is detrimental to our health. The people who lived in the midst of warm, healthy relationships lived longer and the healthy relationships proved to be more protective.

Once the subjects were in their 80s, the study ran prediction algorithms on who would turn out healthier and live longer, from the age of 50. It wasn't their cholesterol levels that determined who would live longer, but it was the people who had closer, more meaningful and cherishable relationships. The people who reported having good, closer relationships were the healthiest at age 80.

3. Good relationships don't just protect our bodies but they protect our minds

Good relationships buffer us from some of the slings and arrows of getting old. It turns out that being in a securely attached relationship to another person in your 80s makes the brain healthier. The people who reported being in more meaningful relationships with their partners and families had sharper memories and had healthier brains than those that reported otherwise.

As Robert Waldinger, the fifth director of this monumental study, shared in his TED Talk, these insights remind us of an age-old truth often overshadowed by the hustle for success: relationships shape not only our present well-being but our future.

In a culture focused on achievements, relationships might feel like a given, something we can relegate to the background & peripheries of our lives while we pursue more "tangible" goals.

But it's through relationships that life finds meaning; through our bonds with others, & the deep connections we establish. Furthermore, our relationships nurture good health & our wellbeing. So perhaps the way to live richly isn't just by striving for our life goals & career milestones but by connecting deeply with our family & friends.

About Coping with Loss

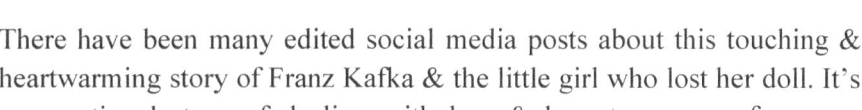

There have been many edited social media posts about this touching & heartwarming story of Franz Kafka & the little girl who lost her doll. It's an emotional story of dealing with loss & how to recover from any significant loss in your life.

As the story goes, at 40, Franz Kafka (1883-1924) the famous Czech novelist & writer came across a little girl in Steglitz Park in Berlin. The little girl was crying her eyes out because she had lost her favourite doll.

Seeing the distraught little girl in the park, Kafka decided to intervene & entertain her & began to help the girl find the doll. After searching for some time, Kafka told the little girl to meet him in the same park the very next day and they would look for the doll again.

After Kafka returned home, a brilliant idea struck him & so he wrote a letter pretending to be from the doll & met the child the next day. After another unsuccessful search attempt at finding the missing doll, Kafka gave the girl the letter pretending it was written by the doll that read, "Please don't cry. I took a trip to see the world. I will write to you about my adventures."

This started a series of several meetings between Kafka & the little girl towards the end of his life. Kafka would meet the little girl regularly & read out letters supposedly written by the doll with elaborate adventures, stories and conversations which the girl adored & looked forward to each day.

Finally, Kafka bought another doll from a store in Berlin & gifted the little girl the new doll saying her old doll had returned.

However, after looking at the doll the little girl said, "It doesn't look like my doll at all."

Kafka gave the girl another note saying, "My travels have changed me." The girl immediately hugged the new doll & took her happily back home full of love & excitement that her beloved doll had returned from her adventures. A year later Kafka died. He didn't marry or have children either.

Several years after Kafka's death, the little girl, then an adult, found a little note inside the new doll signed by Kafka that read, "Everything you love will probably be lost, but in the end, love will return in another way."

There are some lessons we can learn from this touching story. Loss is almost certain in the passageways of life & at some stage, we all grapple with loss. But here's how we can prepare ourselves to cope with it & live a more fulfilled life. Here are some takeaways we can learn from this heartwarming yet tragic story.

Lessons We Can Learn From The Story Of Kafka, The Girl & The Doll

Life Is Too Short

Kafka's own life was a fleeting one; he died young at 40, plagued by illness.

Perhaps it was this awareness that led him to pause his daily routine to comfort the little girl. Life moves with a relentless momentum, and in its brevity, there's an invitation to cherish each moment, each connection, each gesture of kindness. The world can be overwhelming, especially in moments of loss, but if we remember that our time here is limited, then our choices—how we treat others, what we hold onto, what we let go—begin to matter more deeply.

Kafka's act reminds us that even a simple gesture of kindness can be a powerful way to live in life's impermanence.

Traveling Helps in Personal Growth

The doll's "journey" serves as a subtle nod to the transformative power of travel, as I've explored in the earlier chapter. In Kafka's story, the doll's absence was reimagined as an adventure, one that brought growth, new experiences, and transformation. When we travel, we leave behind our comfort zones, confronting new situations, new people, and new ways of thinking. Loss can sometimes propel us into our own journey, pushing us out of familiar spaces into territories that challenge us. Whether it's moving to a new city, taking a solo trip, or even exploring new ideas, each journey shapes us, making us more resilient and open to life's uncertainties.

Loss Is Certain, But Love and Peace Come with Time

The ache of loss is universal; we're all bound to face it at some stage of our lives. But Kafka's approach to the girl's sorrow, rather than erasing it, gently reframed it. He didn't deny her grief, but instead, he acknowledged it and found a way to soften its edges, allowing healing to take root over time. Loss doesn't dissipate overnight — it lingers, reshaping itself, until, eventually, peace emerges, often in unexpected ways. Through Kafka's letters, the girl came to terms with her doll's absence, finding a new perspective on her love and loss.

Time is an unseen healer, and in time, our sorrow gives way to acceptance and, peace. As the famous actor Joaquin Phoenix stated in his Oscar acceptance speech quoting his late brother River, "Run to the rescue with love & peace will follow."

Embrace the Unknown: It's Where Growth Happens

In telling the little girl that her doll had gone off to see the world, Kafka opened her to the vast, mysterious beauty of the unknown. Life is full of uncertainties, of things we can't control, understand, or anticipate. And yet, it's precisely in that ambiguity that we find the most room to grow. By accepting the unknown and allowing ourselves to explore it—whether it's through change, loss, or simply trying something new—we become more comfortable with life's natural ebb and flow. Embracing uncertainty can be unsettling, but it's also where growth happens and where, like Kafka's doll, we find new stories and parts of ourselves.

Storytelling as Healing

Kafka's approach to the girl's loss wasn't to offer solutions but to tell a story—a comforting one, gently layered with the magic of imagination. In reframing her loss through letters, he allowed the girl to reimagine her reality, transforming her grief into something that could be explored, softened, and eventually accepted. Stories have a unique way of helping us cope, of providing a framework through which to understand our feelings and experiences. When we lose something or someone, sometimes the most healing thing we can do is give that loss a new narrative, one that doesn't erase the pain but helps us live with it in a way that fosters acceptance, resilience, learning and meaning.

So if you've lost someone dear to you, remember stories & moments with them, those that you can remember them for. Tell stories of the person(s) you've lost to your loved ones, and recount their charm, love, wit & lessons. In remembering them through the lens of telling stories about them, it's a loving & healing way to gracefully & slowly let go of your loss & remember them for their good parts & the heartwarming times you spent with them.

Remember all the good times & cherishable moments you spent with them & what they said to you & taught you throughout your life.

Kafka's encounter with the girl and her doll reminds us of our shared humanity and the gentle ways in which we can support one another. Life is filled with changes and goodbyes, with losses both big and small.

But when we come together, sharing stories, offering comfort, allowing ourselves to feel and to grow, we find the strength to navigate the road ahead, and also to cherish the journey of life itself.

Live By a Code

*"You, you are on the road, must have a code that you can live by.
And so, become yourself because the past is just a goodbye"*
— *Crosby, Stills, Nash & Young*

The concept of 'dharma' as explored in Eastern philosophy, is well documented. 'Dharma' translates to 'duty' & a key or core element that proceeds your duty is the code you live by. During my school days, we had a class called 'Value Ed' or 'Value Education', which essentially was a class that instilled values into our psyche & value system. The class was particularly unique to my school, & despite a band of us sneaking behind the sheds that aligned the perimeters our school's football ground to smoke a few cigarettes for the first time, that particular class was to encourage developing our own code that we could live by.

As the years pass & you mature, there's a lot of stuff that's good & bad. But to bracket & bucket everything into good & bad or grey areas is of course a futile attempt at being righteous. Pink Floyd's lyrics in their hit song 'Money' from *Dark Side of The Moon* perhaps echoes this, where Roger Waters sings "Money it's a hit! Don't give me that do goody-good bullshit".

But despite the race for the buck, having a code you can follow & adhere to makes you the person you are. It's not about good or bad or right & wrong it's about doing the things & upholding ideas that define you, as a person. It's the value system & moral ethical code you live by.

Having a code can be anything. It's usually about who you innately are. You set your own code & live upto it. It can be anything from learning from a mistake & not repeating it, some core ideals about life or where you draw the line.

A code can also be thought as your own policies towards yourself & towards others. This can be towards your family, children, or at the workplace or towards strangers. It's also your ethics & your values.

Your code is also a defining strand in the grand fabric of your personality & make-up. It's not something you portray for society but part of your own internal & innate make-up & the way you behave in the world, whether that's in facing adversity or simply navigating through life.

So, live by a code, whatever it may be to you.

In The End, It Doesn't Matter Whether You Get Rich or Not But How Fulfilled Your Life Is

"I think everybody should get rich and famous and do everything they ever dreamed of, so they can see that it's not the answer." - Jim Carrey

It's a rat race everywhere you go. There's this constant need to chase money & accrue wealth and become rich, but in the process, we forget to live. Capitalism has its pros and cons — unchecked capitalism has done its own share of damage to the planet as we grapple with global warming and climate change.

However, from a philosophical perspective, capitalism does give us purpose, and a "why" as we live our daily lives.

Everybody wants to get rich, but is it really the answer? People who aren't rich, think that accumulating a lot of money is the answer to all their problems.

While on the other side of the coin, there are multitudes of rich and wealthy people who are unhappy, not at peace & have their own set of problems that they're dealing with.

Money brings comfort & peace of mind. That's perhaps the most valuable aspect about having money. But if you have enough to live comfortably, then why put your peace, health & the simple joys and process of living your life in the balance, just to make more wealth?

Oftentimes, rich and famous people have no privacy & are constantly followed, chased and haggled everywhere they go by paparazzi, reporters & fans.

Something as common as simply walking down the street or going to the supermarket or going anywhere for that matter becomes an ordeal for most famous people, and they covet the privacy that regular folk have.

It's a rather comical paradox: the rich want the simple things that non-rich people have, while the not so rich people want the luxuries that rich & famous folk have.

Whether you're rich or not, there will always be problems and trials & tribulations, and time is your most valuable resource. Trading in your time in a constant cycle to chase and accumulate more wealth each day can be counterproductive and could also be detrimental to your health.

Our time is limited, elucidated by the first chapter — 4000 weeks— so what we do with it is perhaps the most vital aspect of living life. If, for example, you have a 3 to 4 hour work day and work remotely, wherein you can travel to any place in the world with a pristine view and work and make enough, that's such a fulfilling way to work and live your life.

Sure it's nice to have a lot of money, and the comfort it brings, but if you have enough for a roof over your head, food, and enough to take care of your family, and enough buffer in your bank account then there's no need for ignoring & putting aside what you have, in order to chase something you don't have & in the process forget to live your life to the fullest.

How much is enough? Well, that's a subjective question and only you can answer it. You still have to do your duties of providing for your family, educating your kids and having enough to live everyday comfortably, which is what you need to work towards.

In the process of trying to make more money & the greed that the desire to become richer entails, we lose our ethics, our peace of mind, and forget where we've come from & our principles; it's all an unnecessary struggle for something that is immaterial when you eventually die.

On your death bed, you'll be forced to sign papers & documents as you're slowly dying so that your wealth can be transferred to someone else, whether it's your family or relatives or others. At that point, if you're super rich, nobody will care that you're about to die, they'll just be fighting over the possession of your assets.

Make Your Own Waves

To spend all that time and all those moments and resources on simply accumulating money, only to have nobody care about you while you're dying, and trying to take what you spent your entire life dedicated to achieving for themselves instead of loving & caring about you in your final moments; what an irony of life that is.

In the end you still live out your life whether you're rich or not. So, it's important to live it out to the fullest.

A simple family vacation, celebrating a birthday, or a festival or holiday, traveling somewhere with a beautiful view, enjoying and spending time with the one's you love, living and taking pauses and just immersing ourselves in the entire living experience, is so much better than the stress and the constant need to accrue more wealth.

If that's your ultimate goal in life, i.e. to become the wealthiest you can possibly be, by all means pursue it, but understand that you're trading your time in for it; time that you'll probably never get back.

Just as actor Jim Carrey elucidates — even if you get everything you've ever dreamed about, you'll find that it's not the answer.

In the end, it doesn't matter in the grander purpose of your existence, it's the little things — how you live each day & the lives you touch, the change you usher & how you live your life & live out your life's purpose.

So, in the end, it really doesn't matter whether you get rich or not, it's about how you spend your 4000 weeks.

Leave A Legacy

As this book comes to an end, as I write the final chapter, there's something that lingers beyond the final page & beyond any last words or insights. It's the idea of *legacy*—the traces of ourselves that ripple in the fabric of time after we're gone. Legacy isn't just about wealth, fame, or accomplishments. It's a reflection of our values, our connections, and the impact we've had on others. It's the stories people will tell about us, the changes we inspired, and the ways in which we enriched the lives of those around us.

This book was written with the premise to encapsulate all the ideas & knowledge I've come across over the years to share with the collective so that it might educate, heal, empower, help & inspire someone somewhere down the line.

Throughout these chapters, we've navigated the winding paths of self-discovery, resilience, growth, and understanding. Each concept explored herein—whether it was learning to live in the moment, striving for balance, or embracing change—feeds into the larger journey of leaving a meaningful legacy. A legacy isn't built in a day or a moment; it's the cumulative effect of daily actions, small decisions, and personal commitments. When we live aligned with our purpose & values and make choices that reflect our authentic selves, we are continuously building our legacy.

So how do you want to be remembered? This is a question that may take years, or even a lifetime, to fully answer, but it's also a question we answer each day in the way we live. It's in the kindness we extend, the patience we practice, the dreams we pursue, and the courage we muster when we step on the roads less traveled.

Make Your Own Waves

The beauty of legacy is that it's personal & yet part of the collective; it doesn't demand that we be larger-than-life figures or that we accomplish monumental feats. It only requires us to be intentional, to live with purpose, and to be fully present & helpful. We create our legacy in the way we impact others, not just in what we achieve for ourselves.

Leaving things behind, whether they're creative pursuits or creative outlets we've explored & created that will outlast us, or acts of generosity, all add up.

They also are definitely a way to connect with someone, somewhere down the line in time who resonates with what we've created — leading to a eureka moment where they can say, "Oh, yes, I get that" or "Oh, this has helped me," that itself stands the test of time & is a testament to human ingenuity & ideas.

But legacy is not only confined to the things we leave behind; it's also the hope, inspiration, and love we instil in others. It's a reminder that, while our time here is finite, our influence endures.

And as I close the final chapter of this book, let's carry forward the ideas mentioned in the pages of this little book, that will help in creating lives that resonate with purpose, compassion, and integrity.

In the end, it's about living well and it's about leaving a mark that echoes with the best parts of ourselves & touches the lives of others.

So go ahead, and make your own waves…

www.ingramcontent.com/pod-product-compliance
Lightning Source LLC
LaVergne TN
LVHW041840070526
838199LV00045BA/1370